Frank Sinatra & Dean Martin: Show Business Icons

By Charles River Editors

About Charles River Editors

Charles River Editors was founded by Harvard and MIT alumni to provide superior editing and original writing services, with the expertise to create digital content for publishers across a vast range of subject matter. In addition to providing original digital content for third party publishers, Charles River Editors republishes civilization's greatest literary works, bringing them to a new generation via ebooks.

Introduction

Frank Sinatra (1915-1998)

"May you live to be 100 and may the last voice you hear be mine." – Frank Sinatra

America has always celebrated its star entertainers, but Frank Sinatra remains a unique American legend. A pop culture fixture for over half a century, Sinatra's music is still cherished, and his persona remains its own archetype of the quintessential American star. Sinatra transcended genres to the extent that his music stands alone as its own kind of American music, with songs like "New York, New York," "Chicago," and "Come Fly With Me" instantly recognizable among all Americans.

Of course, there was also the life that went with the music. The cultural identity of the Rat Pack, epitomized in the 1960 film Ocean's Eleven, further contributed to his fame, and everyone knows and appreciates the image of easy living, smooth voice and exuberant starpower that Sinatra represents. If anything, Sinatra's ability to make so many people feel happy and good about themselves was one of the main ingredients of his success. And as evidence of the fact that

Americans don't mind their stars doing a little dirt, Sinatra's rap sheet and relationship with the mob are practically a celebrated part of his life.

Given his almost universal appeal, it is easy to forget that Sinatra did not always enjoy strong popularity during his career. He had a meteoric rise to fame, but he also suffered a terrible mid-career slump in popularity and was forced to work hard to reinvent his public image. In a sense, the many changes to his public identity only make him even more American; the American public loves an underdog figure, and during his rise back to fame Sinatra came to embody the struggling American hero. The many transformations that Sinatra made throughout his career were necessary to cement his legacy as an unshakeable American icon.

Show Business Icons looks at the life, career and legacy of Ol' Blue Eyes. Along with pictures of important people, places and events in his life, you will learn about Sinatra like never before.

Dean Martin (1917-1995)

"If people want to think I get drunk and stay out all night, let 'em. That's how I got here, you know." – Dean Martin

   Like Frank Sinatra, Dean Martin is an American legend for his longevity and success across a garden variety of different platforms. Martin began as a nightclub singer, performed in a comedy act, starred in films, recorded hit albums, and capped his career by serving as a television host. In fact, there may be no star who was better able to transcend the different avenues of entertainment.

Martin's success was made all the more amazing by the fact that he never had to change his personality or persona to find success in his different endeavors. From the beginning, Martin's public persona remained largely unchanged. He grew more famous and wealthy, but he always remained the smooth-talking Italian with the easy charm and the cool veneer. As Jerry Lewis noted in his memoirs about Martin, "Dean had this uncanny way of making everything bad look like it wasn't all that bad." If anything, Martin suggested that no matter the circumstances, people can always face their situation with leisurely charm.

   Martin's versatility is unprecedented even today, an era in which stars routinely alternate between film and musical careers. Martin was able to simultaneously work across different media at the same time; even after rising to fame as a singer, he continued to perform with Jerry

Lewis and star in films. But after his film career took off, he continued to perform the crooning style of music that had made him famous and had long since been outdated. While other actors were forced to drastically alter their persona to keep up with the times, Martin's ability to fuse suave glamour with an everyday ordinariness ensured he didn't need to transform anything.

Martin's life and career are often compared to his close friend and contemporary Frank Sinatra, and for good reason. Both came from proud Italian families, both were cohorts in the famed Rat Pack in the 1960s, and they each maintained success even late in their careers. However, Sinatra's career was filled with far more ups and downs than Martin, and his public image experienced highs and lows along with it. It's also somewhat ironic that it was Martin who Anglicized his name but remained a bigger Italian icon than Sinatra. They each began their careers as Italian crooners, but Martin maintained his style while Sinatra adopted a brasher, more "All-American" singing method. Martin never strayed far from his humble background, even as he became one of America's biggest stars.

Show Business Icons profiles the life and career of one of America's most famous performers. Along with pictures of important people, places, and events, you will learn about Dean Martin like never before.

Frank Sinatra

Chapter 1: An Italian Dandy on the Streets of New Jersey

"People often remark that I'm pretty lucky. Luck is only important in so far as getting the chance to sell yourself at the right moment. After that, you've got to have talent and know how to use it." – Frank Sinatra

Frank Sinatra was born on December 12, 1915 in Hoboken, New Jersey. As his last name would suggest, he was born to Italian parents: Antonino Martino Sinatra and Natalie Garaventa (who also went by the names Dolly and Della). They were Italian immigrants, and Frank was their only child. One of the more unusual aspects of Sinatra's family is that Frank would not go by the same last name as his parents. During the early part of the 20th century, Italian-Americans did not enjoy the same level of cultural assimilation and tolerance as Irish-Americans, so Antonino went by the name Marty O'Brien. This created an odd dynamic, because Dolly and Marty proudly raised their child in the Italian Roman Catholic tradition even as they presented themselves as Irish-Americans. Frank was raised to take pride in his Italian heritage and always maintain a strong sense of self-confidence.

Antonino Martin Sinatra

Dolly and Antonino were a study in contrasts. Frank's mother was considerably bolder and more driven than her husband. The two had met in New Jersey at a very young age; Dolly was just 16 years of age when she met Antonino and immediately fell in love with him. Frank's father was just 18 years old himself at the time, and the mutual attraction between the two was forbidden by their families. Antonino's family was from Sicily and Dolly's family hailed from Genoa, leading to a mutual dislike among their families. It ultimately forced the young couple to elope. Frank's parents married two years after meeting each other at the City Hall in Jersey City.

Eventually, Dolly and Antonino reconciled with their parents, but the reasons for doing so were out of necessity. Antonino was trying to forge a professional boxing career, and he was a skilled athlete, but he wasn't making enough money to provide for his family. The young couple had to rely on their parents.

Dolly and Antonino relocated to a tenement flat at 415 Monroe Street in Hoboken, New Jersey, where they would live for several years. Needing to find gainful employment, Dolly found her husband work at the local fire department, where he would eventually progress to the rank of crew chief. Meanwhile, Dolly was active in the Democratic Party and supplemented her husband's income by performing illegal abortions and serving as a midwife. On weekends, she also took a position in a candy store, where she primarily dipped chocolates. It was only after several years did they decide to change their name; needing to make more money, they purchased a saloon and named it "Marty O'Brien's". From that point forward, Antonino was known as Marty O'Brien.

On the outside, Antonino would have fit the stereotype of the rough Irishman. He had fought as a boxer until injuries forced him to stop, his arms were covered in tattoos, and his side job with the fire department only enhanced his hardy image. At the same time, however, Antonino was dominated by his mother, in clear defiance of the traditionally patriarchal gender dynamics of Italian culture. He was a shy, illiterate man who before opening the bar had perpetual difficulty securing lasting employment. He took work as a chauffeur but was unable to sustain the position. Moreover, his asthma and the physical injuries he had received during his boxing career made his health more fragile than it would appear at first glance. Despite the tough exterior, it seems he was a gentle, lighthearted man who was dominated by his fiery, ambitious wife, who would disguise herself as a man to watch her husband box.

Even from this quick glimpse of Frank's parents, several defining attributes are noticeable. The most noticeable and noteworthy characteristic of Frank's parents was his mother's stubbornness. She married her husband over the objections of her parents when she was still a teenager. She was also the driving force behind the family's finances, pushing and prodding her husband to various jobs. For people with such distinctive pride in their home country, it is remarkable that Frank's parents would go to the lengths of presenting Antonino as an Irishman and profiting from the ostensibly Irish enterprise of Marty O'Brien's Bar. However, they held a firm desire for upward mobility, and they were even willing to subdue their Italian heritage in the interests of progressing through the ranks of early 20th century New Jersey society.

In that regard, purchasing an Irish bar made perfect sense. They took over the bar during Prohibition, a time in which saloonkeepers stood to earn lucrative profits from alcohol-thirsty citizens. Furthermore, Hoboken during this time was a seedy town replete with mob affiliations, and with the proper connections it was not difficult to find alcohol. Legendary gangsters like Meyer Lansky, Bugsy Siegel, Joe Adonis, Johnny Torio, Frank Costello, and Lucky Luciano frequented Hoboken with some regularity. Naturally, both of Dolly's brothers, Dominick and Lawrence, had strong ties with the mob, which helped supply Dolly and her husband with their alcohol. Dominick was a welterweight boxer who hijacked whiskey with the famous gangster Dutch Schultz. As a result, Marty O'Brien's was regularly visited by members of the mob and enjoyed steady business.

Given her no-nonsense disposition, a lot people would get the impression that Dolly would have desired a son, but she had always wanted a daughter. In fact, she was disappointed to give birth to a son, and she was fond of dressing Frank in girls' clothing during his early years. At a time in which it was common for people to have large families, the logical solution to her predicament would have been to have more children, but there were complications associated with Frank's birth that dissuaded Dolly from giving birth once again. Frank nearly died from the experience, and he was left with a scarred face and damage to his ear. His left ear had a bifurcated lobe, leaving it with the appearance of having been smashed. Eventually, he would have a mastoid operation on it, which left a heavy scar behind the ear. Given the lasting difficulty Frank would have in hearing through his left ear, it is ironic that he was so drawn to music. Dolly was just 19 years old when giving birth, and it is possible that had she been older she would have been better equipped to deal with the harsh effects that resulted. However, she was traumatized by the experience, so she refused to have more children.

Frank and his mother

The decision to have an only child doesn't raise eyebrows today, but it was practically unprecedented in an Italian family of the early 20th century, further demonstrating Dolly's independent streak. And naturally, since Frank was an only child, Dolly had a unique if not overbearing relationship with her son. On the one hand, she doted on him, purchasing elaborate outfits and indulging him with a wardrobe that exceeded their financial means at the time. But Dolly also expected great things from Frank and was harsh with him when he did not meet her expectations. She frequently beat him with a rod and allegedly pushed him down a flight of stairs on one occasion. She was also so busy in the community that she routinely left Frank with his grandmother or with a neighbor. Ultimately, Frank received a very mixed set of messages from his mother. She rewarded him with more than he could ask for, but she also punished him for every transgression. Frank later remembered, "When I got out of hand, she would give me a rap with that little club, then she'd hug me to her breast." One of Frank's friends vouched for Frank, calling his mother "a great big bossy lady, very domineering, scare you to death."

The Sinatra household was not limited to Frank and his parents. Antonino's cousin, Vincent Mazola, joined the household prior to the purchase of the family saloon. The reasons for Vincent's move remain unclear, especially since it came just as Antonino had broken both of his wrists and couldn't work as a boxer or at his primary job as a boilermaker. But even though he was not physically disabled, Vincent was mentally unfit to live on his own and relied on Dolly's authoritative instinct. It may simply have been that only Dolly could handle Vincent. She found him employment working on the docks, although there were limits to her benevolence, as she forced him to hand over his weekly earnings to help defray the cost of rent.

Although they began with no money, Frank's parents quickly rose through the ranks of Hoboken society. The saloon thrived during Prohibition, and the family was able to move out of the low-rent apartment at 415 Monroe Street and into a more desirable 3-bedroom apartment on Willow Avenue. During this time, Dolly also made sure that Frank's appearance befitted that of an upscale child; at a young age, she supplied him with a charge card at department stores and ensured he always possessed a full wardrobe of outfits. Even at a young age, Frank had a strong fashion sense. While other children wore any outfit they could, careful deliberation went into young Frank's appearance.

Given the fact that Frank was the son of a boxer and a strong-willed woman, it seems strange that Dolly raised her son to be what could accurately be called a dandy. The outfits Frank wore reflected the wealth of his parents, but they did not bestow Frank with any credibility on the streets of Hoboken, where he had to spend a lot of his time. Frank was dressed so well that the neighborhood boys went from calling him Scarface to calling him Slacksey.

Even if he didn't dress differently, Frank likely would have been a social outcast in Hoboken. His physical stature was anything but intimidating; Frank would top out at 5'7 and he was painfully skinny, exhibiting an almost androgynous appearance that would remain with him well into adulthood. While Frank liked to talk up the tough streets of Hoboken and claimed he walked around with a lead pipe, the kids who lived there would later remember that he was wholly incapable of being anything like a fighter or scrapper. On top of that, Frank was extraordinarily emotional, a trend that would also remain with him his entire life. His rapid shifts in temperament were frowned upon in a street culture where boys were encouraged to keep their feelings to themselves. Even when Frank tried to buy friendship by giving kids money on the block, he was constantly derided for something.

Frank may not have thrived on the streets of Hoboken, but he loved being in his parents' saloon, which also exposed him to a culture of music that immediately drew him in. When he was especially young, Frank was monitored by either his grandmother or a Jewish neighbor who taught him Yiddish, but as he got older, he was allowed to sing in the bar for tips. Frank would stand on the counter and sing before the bar's patrons, which helped familiarize him with the intricacies of performing before a live audience. Considering how his career turned out, it's no stretch to say that his experiences in his parents' saloon served him better than his classes.

Frank as a boy

Of course, Frank's mixed academic record chagrined his mother. He progressed adequately through elementary and middle school, but he never embraced the classroom environment. At his mother's insistence, he continued to attend as a teenager, and after he graduated from David E. Rue Junior High School, Dolly bought him a used Chrysler convertible for $35. The car was supposed to motivate Frank to pursue his high school studies with greater diligence, yet his mother's wishes were not reciprocated. Frank did manage to enroll at Demarest High School, but his continued inability to adhere to classroom protocol resulted in his expulsion after just 45 days of class. Frank later tried to boast that he was too rowdy for school, but either way, the 14 year old was now out of school and lacked an academic background.

That said, it's important to remember that the situation Frank found himself in was far different than today's high school dropouts. The importance of a high school education was becoming increasingly valued, but it was not necessarily a prerequisite to economic success. Neither of Frank's parents were well-educated, and the academic system during Frank's youth simply did not go well with his personality. Additionally, forms of technology were emerging in the public sphere, and Frank had a keen interest in radio and cinema; in fact, he was one of the few kids who had his own radio. However, it would still be decades before technology was integrated into the classroom, and it's possible that Frank could have found schools today that would have rewarded his musical talents and allowed him to specialize in fine arts. In the 1920s and 1930s, however, high schools had little room for Frank's artistic interests.

Even if Frank was a better student, he had the kind of personality that would have irritated any teacher. Frank was a cocky teenager, in part to overcompensate for his lack of size, and also due to the fact his mother told him to assert his personality. Even though she was irate with her son after his expulsion, there's no question that his irascible personality was a direct result of the values Dolly had impressed upon her son. The way she treated him instilled Frank with a sense of entitlement, and even though she had tried to force her son to work harder in school, bestowing him with lavish gifts like the car inevitably distracted Frank from committing himself to his studies.

Although she had often indulged him too heavily, Dolly also made it clear to her son that he had to get a job. She had dreamed of her son being a doctor or a skilled professional, and it had gone by the wayside before Frank was even an adult. At one point, Dolly screamed at Frank, "If you think you're going to be a goddamned loafer, you're crazy!" But Frank didn't have the work ethic to match his mother's ambition or his own sense of entitlement. Performing menial jobs forced him to swallow his pride; he accepted a job as a delivery boy for the local newspaper after his mother forced a relative to take the teenager on, but he had difficulty motivating himself to show up to work at such a non-prestigious position. In one bizarre turn of events, a sportswriter for the local paper died suddenly after being hit by a car, and Dolly prodded Frank into trying to take the writer's position, unbeknownst to the supervisors. When they found Frank sitting in a place where he clearly didn't belong, they "fired" him, which set Frank off, hearing of the news, Frank was fired from the job and became enraged. Forever ambitious, his mother attempted to persuade the newspaper official to hire her son, but to no avail.

After losing his newspaper job, Frank explored other opportunities. For three days, he worked at a shipyard, but he could take no more. After that, he was employed by a Manhattan publishing office, but that position was short-lived as well. Finally, he worked on the local docks, cleaning and removing parts of condenser units. This occupation would have been especially difficult to take, both for Frank and his mother, because Frank was working in the same arena as his uncle, a man who was unable to live life on his own.

In a sense, working on the docks represents the nadir of his Frank's life story; he was stuck in a blue-collar job that was entirely antithetical to his personality and dreams. But it did have at least one advantage; the sight of the scrawny boy working at a shipyard also made clear to Frank's parents that their son was not destined to work at a typical masculine form of employment. Frank would show up for work on the dock while wearing a white yachting hat and smoking a pipe, a form of tribute to his idol Bing Crosby, but most boys Frank's age wouldn't have dared wearing such an un-masculine hat. It looked even more absurd at the docks, where it indicated just how out of place the hat and its owner were in a blue-collar position.

Bing Crosby

The boys weren't the only ones who hated the yachting hat. When Dolly saw a picture of Bing Crosby in Frank's room, she allegedly threw a shoe at him. Out of frustration, and in a rare act of assertion, Antonino kicked his son out of the house when Frank was 17. Of course, he was unable to sustain himself and returned home shortly thereafter. Realizing that pursuing a career as a musical performer was fast becoming one of Frank's only remaining options, his parents finally embraced his chosen path. Dolly supplied Frank with enough money to buy a microphone, and she forcefully convinced Joseph Samperi, the owner of the Union Club, to hire Frank as a singer.

Chapter 2: That's Entertainment

"Throughout my career, if I have done anything, I have paid attention to every note and every word I sing - if I respect the song. If I cannot project this to a listener, I fail." – Frank Sinatra

Frank was fortunate to get the job at the Union Club, and it was a reputable establishment that provided him with a more upscale audience than his early years singing at his parents' saloon. As someone who had begun singing as a young child, the job was exponentially more appropriate than working on a dock, and a much better fit for a dandy at that. Still, singing before an audience posed real challenges for Frank at first, especially because he was prone to bouts of stage fright. His body hadn't fully matured yet either, making it more difficult for him to fully project his voice. Even in middle age, Sinatra was never able to develop broad shoulders, and his gangly physique kept his voice shallow. Still, his voice was graceful and, perhaps more importantly, even at a young age he had charisma.

Despite being physically underdeveloped, Frank was very interested in girls from a young age. While that was not ignoble in and of itself, it would be to his detriment later in life. In 1929, he met Nancy Barbato, a neighborhood girl from a respectable Italian family. Although it would be several years before they began dating, they had a strong mutual attraction, and Nancy did not hold his academic or employment failures against him. Indeed, every indication suggests that she was attracted to his ambition and precocious show business talent. But Nancy's parents were unimpressed with their daughter's choice, making the relationship between Frank and Nancy ironically similar in some respects to the one between Frank's own parents. Just as Dolly's parents did not approve of her boyfriend, Nancy's father frowned on his daughter's relationship with a young man who had proven himself entirely unable to secure any manner of lasting employment. It didn't help that show business was not considered a true profession in those days, and with few exceptions, entertainers did not command the robust salaries that they would begin receiving in the years to come. With the benefit of hindsight, it is easy to criticize his ambivalence, but he certainly seemed fully justified at the time considering Frank a lazy kid who would be incapable of supporting a large Italian family. And in some respects, he would be proven correct.

Frank remained in his position at the Union Club for an extended period of time, and it is possible that he would have remained there for many years had it not been for his mother's intervention. Just as she had been responsible for his getting hired at the Union Club, she would play an integral role in Frank receiving his first major break. In 1935, a trio of singers known as the Three Flashes became very popular, and though their success would be short-lived (and make their band name apropos), Dolly knew that if her son joined the group, he would get the popularity he needed to properly establish his own name. She spoke with the group, informing them that her son was gifted enough to join their band. But even if Frank did have the necessary talent, there was little motivation for them to hire a new singer, since profit margins were slim and they were not lacking in popularity themselves. As it turned out, Frank's main selling point had nothing to do with his voice or his charisma. It had everything to do with the fact that he owned a car. The Chrysler was one of the wisest investments his mother ever made, since it was instrumental in Frank being hired to join the group.

Dolly had even greater motives than simply finding a spot for her son in a singing group. She was aware that the Three Flashes had a major audition coming up for the radio personality Major Bowes, who was shooting film shorts at the nearby Biograph studio in the Bronx. If Frank joined the group and was featured in one of the shorts, he would instantly be seen on a grander scale than he could ever have otherwise acquired.

Major Bowes

The audition was a success, and Major Bowes allowed them to appear regularly for his radio show, with the group name changed to the Four Flashes and then the Hoboken Four to reflect the inclusion of their newest member. Each member was signed to a six-month contract to perform onstage, and they toured in a bus and became even more popular. Girls especially loved Frank, who started receiving singing lessons for the first time. Until this point, his technique had been entirely self-taught, and even after his lessons, he continued to have difficulty reading music throughout his career.

Sinatra (far right) singing with the Four Flashes

At the conclusion of the contract, Frank was now well-known but still needed to find employment. To solve this dilemma, he was hired as an MC and waiter at the Rustic Cabin in Englewood Cliffs, New Jersey, where he was paid a mere $15 per week. By today's standards, Frank's job at the Rustic Cabin seems unusual, since it's rare for servers to double as musical performers, but this was not uncommon in the 1930s. Charlie Chaplin played the role of a singing waiter at the end of *Modern Times* (1936). It is also easy to imagine the boyish looking Sinatra as a waiter, since his small stature was well-suited for moving gracefully throughout a dining room.

While at Englewood Hills, Frank's relationship with Nancy Barbato became more serious, and the two settled into a domestic routine. Her parents remained lukewarm about to Frank, but by the late 1930s they had known each other for the better part of a decade. Although it was difficult to survive on Frank's meager salary, Nancy was a skilled cook who learned how to prepare her boyfriend's favorite dishes. Although his salary was barely enough to live on, Frank routinely spent on himself at the expense of his wife, purchasing lavish suits and maintaining a fancy wardrobe even when he could only afford outfits that cost a fraction of the price. Despite Frank's self-centered nature, they married in 1939. The decision to get married was spurred by the fact that Nancy was pregnant.

Frank and Nancy

Although Frank would later show consistent love toward his children, it is worth considering whether he was actually in favor of having the child. Although he would not admit it, there remains the strong possibility that Frank had not wanted to have children, and the birth of his first child was almost certainty unplanned. But Nancy supported the idea of raising a family, as her upbringing had ingrained upon her the philosophy that a woman's role involved caring for children. Even though Frank's family was Italian, he had never truly adhered to masculine roles, and the birth of their daughter Nancy was likely due to cultural pressure more than anything else.

Nancy Sinatra

Also complicating the decision to have a child was the fact that Frank had never been faithful to his wife. In 1938 Frank was arrested on a morals charge after a woman he was having an affair with accused him of breaching a promise to get married. The embarrassing episode brought landed Frank briefly in prison. Frank's famous mugshot is one of the most recognizable pictures he took, but it was simply the result of an adulterous affair.

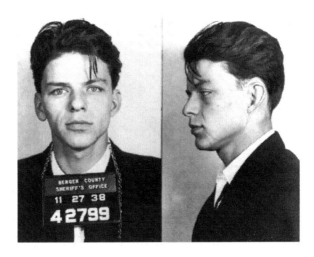

By 1938, Frank had been involved with Nancy for a long time and was growing restless. His job at Englewood Cliffs afforded him the opportunity to meet many women, and he carried on a long affair with a woman named Toni. In a surprising move, he asked her to marry him. Toni was the complete opposite of Nancy, and though he was still fond of his wife, he had grown bored with her and liked the excitement Toni provided. Nancy came from a very conservative and traditional Italian family, and she was simply unwilling to indulge Frank sexually in a way other women would. But Nancy was assertive when she learned her boyfriend had proposed to another woman; she verbally chastised Frank in person and Toni over the phone, then told her husband that he would be remaining with her. It was through this bizarre sequence of events that Frank was arrested on a morality charge brought by Toni. The case did not go anywhere, but the incident is representative of the type of public relations issues that Frank would later suffer after becoming famous.

Frank's arrest occurred in 1938, and it is possible that the decision to get married and have a child was the result of Nancy requiring a commitment from her longtime boyfriend after that embarrassing incident. In any event, while he was willing to submit to raising a family, on a professional level Frank had high ambitions that were not met by working at Englewood Cliffs. Fortunately, he received his second major break in 1940 after the famous singer Harry James watched him perform. Immediately after the performance, he signed Sinatra on the spot, offering him a salary that doubled what he was previously earning. At first, James thought Frank's last name should be changed, but Frank refused and James acquiesced. After that, Frank joined the Harry James Band, a group that travelled throughout the country.

Life with the Harry James band was decidedly unglamorous. The groups travelled by bus, and

Frank had to get accustomed to sleeping on the vehicle. But Frank was rewarded with fame and renown far beyond what he could have found in Englewood Cliffs. Furthermore, life on the road gave him the opportunity to carry on affairs with women that Nancy would never be able to discover. During this period, he also recorded 10 songs, produced by the Brunswick and Columbia labels, the latter of which would prove instrumental later in his career. The majority of these were crooning love ballads that are of little note, but Frank did record one major hit: "All or Nothing at All". That song earned him broad exposure, even though it was different than the kind of hits that people still associate with Sinatra. Still under the influence of James, Sinatra's singing style had little of the brash confidence that would characterize his later style, even if the smoothness with which he could carry a melody was already on display.

Sinatra singing for Harry James

While singing with Harry James and his band, Sinatra was also exposed to a much wider audience than New Jersey. In 1940, while touring in Chicago, Sinatra was discovered by Tommy Dorsey, a famous jazz musician in the big band tradition. Impressed with Frank, Dorsey offered him the opportunity to join his band and lured him with the prospect of $75 per week. That was double what he was making with Harry James, and naturally Frank jumped at the offer, even though he had enjoyed being on the road with James and was sad to leave his cohorts.

Tommy Dorsey

Dorsey was already famous, and the opportunity to sing for his band gave Frank more publicity than ever before. Frank's own popularity exploded, and it was with Dorsey that he began recording the kinds of songs that made him a legend. The crooning melodies he had performed with Harry James were replaced with a brasher, more grandiose style that emphasized having a good time rather than ruing misfortune. Dorsey also became a mentor for Frank, and Sinatra's show business persona, predicated on being smooth and living easy, was largely built around Dorsey. In 1940, Sinatra recorded the hit song "I'll Never Smile Again," which topped the charts for 12 weeks. Another famous song recorded during this period was "Chicago," a brash paean to the Windy City that is now permanently linked with the city. In 1941, Sinatra reached the top position on the male singer polls in Billboard and Downbeat Magazines, making him the most famous singer in the country.

Sinatra and Dorsey in 1941

The shift from the more sorrowful melodies of the Harry James Band to the booming style of the Tommy Dorsey era proved to be exactly what wartime America craved. Audiences were able to forget the dangers overseas, thanks to Sinatra's form of escapist musical entertainment. But like many entertainers and stars, Sinatra drew a great deal of criticism for not actually fighting in the war itself. He had been able to avoid the draft by qualifying as being psychologically unstable. Sinatra could act erratically at times, and he suffered from anxiety, but that was all hidden from the public to protect his image, which gave rise to a widely held belief that he had simply faked his way out of supporting the war effort. While other musicians were fighting overseas, many people thought Sinatra was staying home and enjoying a lack of competition in the industry.

Sinatra being interviewed by the American Forces Network

The criticisms leveled against Sinatra were legitimate, since Sinatra clearly did not want to serve in combat, but he did at least provide a service to soldiers and the public by offering cheerful melodies. Sinatra appealed to both men and women, but he was especially popular with women, and his image was somewhat analogous to the way men thought of Rita Hayworth. Just as Hayworth offered men an image of American glamour during the war, Sinatra was seen the same way by young women, particularly teenagers. At first glance, it may seem surprising that the lanky Sinatra had such sex appeal, since he looked more like a song-and-dance man in the Fred Astaire tradition than a traditionally masculine presence, but he had charisma and a unique style. Audiences simply hadn't heard a voice like his.

Chapter 3: Going Solo

"What I do with my life is of my own doing. I live it the best way I can." – Frank Sinatra

As 1942 progressed, Frank realized that he was now more popular than Dorsey and his band mates, so he took the unusual move of breaking out on his own, despite the fact he did not have a record contract. Moreover, he was still contractually obligated to Dorsey, who knew how to strong-arm Frank like his mother did. Frank's contract required him to turn over 33% of his lifetime earnings to Dorsey, and another 10% to Dorsey's agent. Although he had always gotten along well with Frank, Dorsey was not a benevolent figure, and he was unwilling to allow his star singer to leave his band. The exact means through which Sinatra disengaged himself from Dorsey are steeped in mystery, but legend holds that Sinatra used his connections with the mob to convince Dorsey to let him out of his contract. Sinatra always denied that version of events, but it is not entirely improbable considering the strong mob ties held by his family. According to Sinatra biographer J. Randy Taraborrelli, three gangsters visited Dorsey and "talked out of the sides of their mouths and ordered him to 'sign or else.'" Sinatra had offered $60,000 to Dorsey to let him go, and after that visit, Dorsey reportedly ripped up the contract for $1. One of Dorsey's visitors may have been Hoboken gangster Willie Moretti, who apparently liked to look after his hometown hero.

Sinatra's relationship with the mob is one of the best known aspects of his life, even though the nature of his connection to mob figures remains murky. FBI Director J. Edgar Hoover kept a file on Sinatra and investigated, but aside from noting that Sinatra had friendships with gangsters like Lucky Luciano and Chicago mob boss Sam Giancana, and that he hung out with gangsters on a trip to Cuba, the investigations netted nothing noteworthy. The fact that Sinatra hung out with mobsters wasn't a secret; journalists and photographers often snapped pictures of Sinatra hanging out at clubs with goodfellas.

Sinatra's ties to the mob were popularized by Mario Puzo's *The Godfather* through the character of Johnny Fontane, a crooner who uses his ties to the Corleone family to advance his own career. Fontane is depicted as a hapless figure who can't achieve anything on his own and owes his entire career to his friendships. Sinatra was so disturbed by the implications of the Fontane character that he allegedly confronted Mario Puzo about it. Of course, it's unknown whether Sinatra took offense to the depiction of Fontane being connected with the mob or the fact that Fontane seemed like someone who couldn't make it on his own.

The decision to leave Dorsey was far riskier than it might appear by today's standards. Performers, even famous ones, simply did not go solo. The early 1940s were still a time of big bands and singing quartets, and Frank had little reason to expect that audiences would be drawn to a one-man show. Sure enough, he had great difficulty booking performances until he was able to secure a marquee performance opening the Paramount Theatre in New York City on New Year's Eve in 1942. This was a major event, and Sinatra was to perform after Benny Goodman, an immensely popular singer in his own right.

The performance at the Paramount Theatre is legendary and a milestone even in the broader context of Frank's career. The building was flooded with fans, and after the performance he was mobbed with teenage girls. He would later say, "The sound that greeted me was absolutely deafening. It was a tremendous roar. Five thousand kids, stamping, yelling, screaming, applauding. I was scared stiff. I couldn't move a muscle. Benny Goodman froze, too. He was so scared he turned around, looked at the audience, and said, 'What the hell was that?'"

Sinatra's performance was so successful that he was able to parlay what was originally supposed to be a one-night performance into a longstanding gig that lasted for months. Audiences went nuts, and girls showered him with everything they could get their hands on. Sinatra performed several shows daily, singing from the early morning through late night. On one Saturday, he performed from 8:00 in the morning until 2:00 a.m. that night. Even still, his stamina was exceeded by his fame. A later performance at Paramount Theatre, known today as the "Columbus Day Riot," drew a crowd of over 30,000, and the commotion was so severe that hundreds of policemen were rushed to the scene to moderate the event. Sinatra had reached a level of popularity that had not been witnessed before, and in her memoir, Frank's daughter Nancy wrote that her father was a precursor to James Dean: "When Sinatra played New York's Paramount Theatre in the early 1940s—a skinny kid in his twenties, not long out of Hoboken, New Jersey—he caused the first generation gap. Frank Sinatra sang, teenage girls swooned, and their parents didn't get it."

The description of Sinatra as a magnet to bobbysoxers may seem unlikely, particular since his music is now deployed in more nostalgic contexts and is not often listened to by America's youth. But his newness and infectious energy were exactly what young Americans liked during the War, and even though his image is now somewhat wholesome and American, at the time it was still also considered lively and raw.

Sinatra's lengthy run at the Paramount Theatre proved to be lucrative, but it did not offer him any contractual security. He looked to return to producing records, and in 1943 he signed with Columbia Records as a solo artist. He would remain with the record producer for the remainder of the decade, and while Sinatra's most famous songs would be performed after his time with Columbia, the Columbia years still produced a number of famous recordings. With Columbia, he produced songs like "Close To You," "If You Are But a Dream," and "Why Shouldn't I." His style during this period was not as cheerful as in his later periods, but he continued to perfect the smooth, easy style for which he is famous. He also continued to do live performances, and in 1943 alone he sang at high-profile venues like Madison Square Garden and the Hollywood Bowl.

During the 1940s, Sinatra also tried his hand in the movies. He began his film career with the RKO studio, appearing in *Step Lively* (1944) and *Higher and Higher* (1944). Both were low-budget pictures, and after Louis B. Mayer bought out his contract, Frank signed with MGM. In retrospect, it's remarkable that Sinatra was not immediately signed to a deal with MGM, since that studio was known for musicals and he was America's most famous singer.

After signing with the new studio, Frank appeared with Gene Kelly in the musical *Anchors Aweigh* (1945). As could be expected, the film featured a number of songs performed by the two famous stars, and Frank also proved he was an exceptional dancer. He did not have Gene Kelly's physique, but he carried himself gracefully. Many people have since argued that it was Sinatra's dancing abilities that allowed him to be a movie star, especially during an era when other singers had trouble breaking into the industry.

As Sinatra came of age, he also became more politically active, a byproduct of the fact he was spending more time in Hollywood. His mother was involved with the Democratic Party, and Hollywood was fiercely liberal in the 1940s and 1950s. At the time, Hollywood was a frequent target of politicians at the height of the Red Scare, and stars like Charlie Chaplin were routinely accused of being Communists by the House Committee on Un-American Activities. The Popular

Front, a current of hyper-liberal thought, was just beginning to infiltrate Hollywood and would later contribute to the making of films such as *On the Waterfront* (1953) and *Salt of the Earth* (1954). Sinatra was outspoken in criticizing international figures like Hitler, Franco, and Mussolini, and he served as Vice President of the Hollywood Independent Citizens Committee of the Arts, Sciences, and Professions.

In 1945, Sinatra appeared in the short film *The House I Live In*, in which Sinatra appears with a large group of schoolchildren and preaches the value of racial tolerance. In addition to promoting civil rights, the film covertly aligned Sinatra with the ethos of the Popular Front. Furthermore, it earned Frank significant critical acclaim, winning him the Academy Award for his efforts. Sinatra's role in the film, coupled with his ongoing championing of civil rights, would earn him the Thomas Jefferson Award for Fighting Racial Intolerance in 1947.

Another major development in 1947 was Sinatra's starring role in *It Happened in Brooklyn*, a post-war feel-good story co-starring Peter Lawford, Gloria Graham, and Jimmy Durante. The film was another MGM musical that featured musical numbers like "The Brooklyn Bridge," "Time After Time," and "I Believe." An immensely popular film, it represented the antithesis of the film noirs that were produced during that time. While noir films like *Double Indemnity* (1944) and *Gilda* (1946) reveled in portraying post-war anxiety and masculine discontent, *It Happened in Brooklyn* is much more cheerful. The film is also an example of how stardom was beginning to change at the midpoint of the 20th century. Although there were exceptions, actors and singer-songwriters had existed in their separate domain, but Sinatra's ability to coexist in both and remain a star demonstrated the emergence of a more broad-ranging form of celebrity. Sinatra would pave the way for subsequent crossover stars

Chapter 4: A Career in Decline

"Whatever else has been said about me personally is unimportant. When I sing, I believe. I'm honest." – Frank Sinatra

Although Frank had his fair share of women, his family also grew during the 1940s. In 1944, he and Nancy gave birth to their son Franklin, who was named after President Roosevelt. Their second daughter, Christina, was born in 1948. Obviously, Frank's unparalleled fame made him financially successful above and beyond what was necessary to support his family, but his father-in-law's concern about his ability to be a caring husband and father was well-founded. Sinatra always had difficulty settling into family life, partly because he was constantly on the road but mostly because he was a notorious womanizer.

At times, Frank played along with his reputation, and he was the source of several quotes that today would be deemed misogynist. He also talked about his own reputation, once noting, "I'm supposed to have a Ph.D. on the subject of women. But the truth is I've flunked more often than not. I'm very fond of women; I admire them. But, like all men, I don't understand them." But for someone who had built his reputation on wholesome, cheerful songs that improved the public mood at a time of extreme national conflict, the news of Frank's affairs had a destructive impact on his public image.

Frank's abrasive temper, something he inherited from his mother, was also damaging. But while Dolly's temper had been grudgingly accepted in Hoboken, contemporary American culture held its idols up to a high standard that Frank was unable to meet. He acquired a reputation for lashing out at reporters and media personalities who criticized him or simply failed to treat him with the respect he felt he deserved. An abrasive attitude is more normal today, but in the 1940s, a celebrity simply could not conduct themselves the way Frank did and emerge unscathed.

Sinatra in 1946

Another public relations hit came in 1949 when California Senator Jack B. Tenney revealed a list of celebrities who had been determined to have Communist affiliations. Sinatra's name was featured on the list, alongside luminaries like Gregory Peck, John Garfield, Danny Kaye, and Katherine Hepburn. The FBI kept a file on him for the rest of his life, and it eventually amounted to over 2400 pages. Although he would never be called upon to testify before the House Committee on Un-American Activities, his name popping up on Tenney's list only added to the bad press that had arisen in the preceding years. It is also important to note that the Communist suspicions were particularly destructive for Frank, more so than other actors on the list. For example, Katherine Hepburn had risen to stardom through an assertive public identity that subverted traditional feminine standards, which meant her image was better equipped to deal with the allegations. Frank, on the other hand, was supposed to be a golden boy.

American culture was not ready to accept someone with Frank's temper, but it also had mechanisms in place that would allow him to make a comeback. Still under contract with MGM, Sinatra appeared in a pair of musicals in 1949: *Take Me Out to the Ballgame* and *On the Town*. In both films, Sinatra acted alongside Gene Kelly, reprising the working relationship that had started with *Anchors Aweigh*. Despite the similar casting, the two films Sinatra acted in during 1949 were not at all alike, due to their different directors. *Take Me Out to the Ballgame* was directed by Busby Berkely, a director who adored lavish spectacles and elaborate studio sets at the expense of an engaging narrative. *On the Town* was directed by the more narrative-driven Stanley Donen, who would later direct *Singin' in the Rain* (1952). *On the Town* would turn out to be far more acclaimed than *Take Me Out to the Ballgame*, in part because Sinatra was still skinny and did not possess the athletic build needed to make him look like a baseball player. In *On the Town*, Sinatra and Kelly play sailors who arrive in New York City for 24 hours. The film is an ode to the big city, and it stands as a precursor to Sinatra's famous rendition of "New York, New York".

Sinatra tried to remake his image in the early 1950s by returning to his roots and giving live performances, but the decision didn't work out. He had trouble projecting his voice, and he hemorrhaged his vocal chords during a performance at the Copacabana in April 1950. Eventually he was able to return, and he delivered a number of high-profile performances afterward, but Sinatra's public image had already taken a major hit again. Sinatra was finding it hard to escape the public's belief that he was a washed-up performer who was typically in the headlines for all the wrong reasons. Frank's comeback attempt was ultimately unsuccessful, and in 1950 Louis B. Mayer terminated Sinatra's MGM contract. This situation only got worse in 1952 when Frank was dropped by Columbia. A few years earlier, he was the most famous singer in America, and now he didn't have a studio contract or a record contract. He would need to overhaul his image to reach the top again.

There is no denying that the late 1940s and early 1950s were a difficult time for Sinatra, but there were some satisfying personal developments for Sinatra at the time. In 1951, he married Ava Gardner, the iconic actress and sex symbol whose crude and wild ways were the opposite of his first wife Nancy. When he divorced Nancy, Frank lost custody over his children, but he was madly in love with Ava. Nevertheless, he continued to have too many affairs to count. His charisma helped him attract women almost at will, but it apparently prevented him from being able to sustain his marriages. Ava and Frank were separated in 1953 after less than two years of marriage, and Frank was once again living by himself.

Frank and Ava

Chapter 5: Resurrection

"The big lesson in life, baby, is never be scared of anyone or anything." – Frank Sinatra

Even though Ava was frustrated with her marriage to Frank, she was sympathetic to his floundering career and played an instrumental role in its resurrection. In 1953, Ava was a major star and held significant sway within the industry. The decade was an era of major blockbusters based on big stars, and it was partly in response to the continued threat of television. Aware that a big-budget epic of *From Here to Eternity* was being planned, Ava helped Frank land a supporting role in the film. Released in 1953, *From Here to Eternity* was a war film set in Hawaii in the months preceding the attack by the Japanese on Pearl Harbor. Frank played Angelo Maggio, a private who eventually dies in the arms of his best friend (played by Montgomery Clift). The extremely emotional film, which involved a steamy romance between Burt Lancaster and Deborah Kerr, required a major change in acting style for Sinatra. The cheerful musicals from before were replaced with a brooding disposition that was all the more fitting considering the developments that had taken place in his personal life. Critics and audiences alike applauded his portrayal of the psychologically unstable soldier, and he was awarded the Academy Award for Best Supporting Actor.

A still of Sinatra in *From Here to Eternity*

Sinatra's turn toward a more melancholic acting style was also borne out of the naturalistic acting style being popularized at the time by Marlon Brando, James Dean, Montgomery Clift, and the students who had graduated from Lee Strasberg's Acting Studio. Male actors began to show their emotions, and the turn toward introspection marked a major change, but it was natural for Sinatra, who had always been highly emotional anyway.

The psychological unrest Frank displayed in *From Here to Eternity* became even more pronounced when he starred in *The Man with the Golden Arm* (1955). Directed by Otto Preminger, the film portrayed Frank in the role of Frankie Machine, a heroin addict just released from prison. The film centers on his attempt to stay sober and the pain that he causes to those around him. Always a provocative director, Preminger conveyed drug addiction with an explicitness that had not previously been conveyed on the big screen. Sinatra's character is both infectious and impossible to be around, something that could be said about Sinatra himself. Although the film was not as successful at the box office as *From Here to Eternity*, Sinatra was again praised for his performance. Film critic Pauline Kael noted that "Sinatra's performance is rhythmic, tense, and instinctive, yet beautifully controlled, and of course, he has a performer's presence."

A still of Sinatra in *The Man with the Golden Arm*

Frank's career changed on film, but it was his music career that underwent an enormous renaissance in the 1950s. In 1953, one year after he was dropped by Columbia, Frank signed a seven-year deal with Capitol Records on a meager contract that paid him little and required him to match the recording costs. Undeterred, Frank had a string of hits during the subsequent years. His album *Songs for Young Lovers* reached number three on the charts and included hit songs "I Get a Kick Out of You" and "They Can't Take that Away from Me." That same year, he released *Swing Easy*, which featured his famous rendition of "I'm Gonna Sit Right Down and Write Myself a Letter." The following year was even more lucrative, as he released *In the Wee Small Hours*, which featured a serious of songs centering on loneliness and ennui.

The albums Frank released during the mid-1950s are significant in many ways. First, they were related to both his movie roles and his life at the time. Frank was deeply depressed at the time, and he reportedly attempted suicide at least once. His performances also reflected his uneasy temperament. The albums' songs were also grouped thematically, making him one of the first performers to structure his albums in this way. By focusing on themes, he encouraged the public to view albums as discrete units rather than simply a collection of disparate songs.

Sinatra in 1957

As the 1950s progressed and Frank's musical career once again rose to prominence, his dark style gave way to a more cheerful style that recalled his 1940s recordings. In 1956, he released *Songs for Swingin' Lovers*, an album that featured more upbeat songs like "Pennies from Heaven" and "I've Got You Under My Skin." In 1959, he released *Come Fly with Me*, which reached number one on the charts and stayed there for five weeks. The songs also started exhibiting the extreme confidence Sinatra is famous for today. The next year, he released *Frank Sinatra Sings For Only the Lonely*, which won him the first of many Grammy Awards and which he would later call his favorite album.

At the end of the 1950s, Sinatra became part of the fabled Rat Pack, a group of Hollywood performers who operated in Las Vegas and lived a lavish lifestyle based on heavy drinking and expensive leisure. Although it has since been revealed that there were conflicts within the group, including racism Sinatra directed at Sammy Davis, Jr. by Sinatra himself, the members exuded a powerful public image that helped each of them. Chris Rojek noted:

"Sinatra and the Rat Pack transmitted a generally benign view of masculine domination, a consistently but, for the day, socially acceptable sexist set of attitudes toward women, and a serene introspection in relation to global politics. The public face they concocted of carefree existence, guiltless priapism, easy success, immense wealth, and physical well-being provided a template of cool living."

As this description makes apparent, the Rat Pack era marked a clear turn from the psychologically unstable portrayals Sinatra gave on screen earlier in the decade. Some of Sinatra's most memorable quotes played off this reputation; he would once claim, "For years I've nursed a secret desire to spend the Fourth of July in a double hammock with a swingin' redheaded broad ... but I could never find me a double hammock." Perhaps his most famous quote was, "I feel sorry for people who don't drink. When they wake up in the morning, that's as good as they're going to feel all day."

In 1960, following the conclusion of Sinatra's contract with Capital, the members of the Rat Pack, which included Dean Martin, Sammy Davis, Jr., Joey Bishop, and Peter Lawford, formed Reprise Records. In 1961, Reprise released Sinatra's album *Ring-A-Ding-Ding*, which rose to number four on the charts. The songs featured in the album continued his emphasis on up-tempo songs, highlighted by the album's title song.

Frank Sinatra and Dean Martin

Sinatra's affiliation with the Rat Pack also resulted in film appearances. In 1958, he appeared in Vincente Minnelli's *Some Came Running* (1958), in which he stars as Dave Hirsch, an alcoholic soldier who attempts to return to civilian life and start a career as a writer. Sinatra's character must also contend with the destructive influence of his friend Bama, played by Dean Martin. His love interest in the film is played by Shirley MacLaine, an actress strongly affiliated with the Rat Pack. Independent of the Rat Pack subtext, the film is notable in its own right. The melodramatic film contains a sumptuous visual aesthetic and a heightened emotionalism that is well-suited for Sinatra's expressive acting style.

The most famous Rat Pack film was *Ocean's Eleven*, which starred Sinatra, Peter Lawford,

Dean Martin, Sammy Davis, Jr., and Joey Bishop. The film, which has since been remade, has the Rat Pack starring as casino robbers. Sinatra's role as Danny Ocean cemented his status as the leading member of the group, and it epitomized Sinatra's ability to make illicit behavior attractive.

Throughout the decade, Sinatra began appearing in fewer films, but he did act in *The Manchurian Candidate* (1962), a Korean War film that involves a soldier who suffers from nightmares involving a sadistic fellow soldier. The film recalls the 1940s postwar films that involve soldiers undergoing psychoanalysis, but it is bolder in style.

Meanwhile, Sinatra strengthened his affiliation with the Democratic Party, and he became influenced by folk music. He had always disliked rock music, despite the fact that the rock generation had always appreciated Frank's cocky demeanor. He once called rock music the "most brutal, ugly, desperate, vicious form of expression it has been my misfortune to hear."

Given his dislike for rock, it may seem surprising that he appreciated folk music, but the softer, less abrasive rhythms appealed to him. His commitment to the Democratic Party was tested in 1963, when President Kennedy stayed with him during a vacation, only to leave after hearing of Sinatra's ties to Chicago mob boss Sam Giancana. In fact, the knowledge that Giancana had ties to Frank resulted in Sinatra's gambling license being revoked. This event marked the beginning of Sinatra's incremental turn toward the more conservative Republican Party, but after Kennedy was assassinated, Sinatra recorded the folk-influenced album *America, I Hear You Singing* as a tribute to the slain president.

In 1966, Frank married actress Mia Farrow, and not surprisingly the marriage was troubled from the start. 51 year old Frank was 30 years older than Mia, and Frank acted more like a father than husband. He explicitly disapproved of Farrow's starring role in Roman Polanski's 1968 film *Rosemary's Baby*, in which she played a young woman who has unknowingly conceived of a child with the devil. Even though the film was critically acclaimed, Sinatra's hostility toward the film led to their divorce in 1968.

Even as rock music continued to grow more popular, Sinatra's fame remained intact as well, albeit with his target demographic increasingly becoming older. He continued to release major albums, including *It Might as Well Be Swing*. Released in 1964, which featured songs like "Fly Me to the Moon" and "The Best is Yet to Come". These songs were as brashly confident as any Sinatra song before them. The following year saw the release of *September of My Years,* which reached number five on the charts. He also won a Grammy for his song "It Was a Very Good Year," which reached number one on the charts. As the titles suggest, Sinatra's songs from the 1960s reflect an acknowledgment of his own aging.

Frank may have been getting older, but the late 1960s were every bit as productive as the earlier part of the decade. Frank put out nearly an album a year, including *The World We Knew*

(1967), *Cycles* (1968), and *Watertown* (1970), all of which discuss the trials and tribulations of growing older. His voice grew deeper and more booming, a development that coincided with the thickening of his physique. Whether or not Sinatra was an alcoholic is a topic for debate, but years of hard drinking gave him a bulbous nose and an expanding waistline. Where he had once held a brash facade, his appearance became more paternal, evidenced by his duet with daughter Nancy in 1967's "The World We Knew".

Sinatra officially retired in 1971. He would return to record tracks and perform live on a number of occasions, but he started to scale back his activities significantly in the 1970s and on.

Chapter 6: Later Years

"You gotta love livin', baby, 'cause dyin' is a pain in the ass." – Frank Sinatra

The most significant aspect of Sinatra's life in the late 1960s and early 1970s may have been his shifting political affiliations. Frank had been a diehard Democrat like his mother for all of his life, but he gradually shifted after his fallout with Kennedy. Sinatra's endorsement of Richard Nixon represented the complete political change he underwent, but a lot of people often become more conservative as they grow older, and Sinatra was no exception.

Sinatra with the Nixons in 1973

As he grew older, Sinatra also became increasingly involved in the attempt to reclaim his gambling license, something that took the better part of two decades to complete. In 1981, he was given his license after a long process that required receiving votes of confidence from Gregory Peck, Kirk Douglas, and Bob Hope. His connection with Las Vegas was also strengthened by numerous performances Sinatra gave there after his retirement, highlighted by a high-profile performance at Caesar's Palace in 1974.

Sinatra married for the last time in 1976. This time he married Barbara Marx, whose surname derived from her earlier marriage to legendary Marx Brother Zeppo Marx. Frank's final marriage went far more amicably than his earlier ones, and he and Barbara remained married for the final 22 years of Sinatra's life. Although the marriage went smoothly, Barbara did have a difficult relationship with Frank's children, but Nancy Sinatra also pointed out that many people considered Barbara a difficult woman.

Frank emerged from retirement on a couple of occasions to record. In 1979, he released the album *Trilogy: Past, Present, Future*. The album was mainly comprised of Sinatra's lifetime hits, but it also contained his now legendary performance of "New York, New York." The song might be his most famous today and has come to epitomize Sinatra's style, despite the fact that it was actually written after he had retired. Frank's final recording was with Capitol records in 1993, and he also performed a series of public concerts in 1994. He was given an honorary award at the 1994 Grammy Awards.

Sinatra lived a long life, but in many respects he did not age well. His personality became increasingly difficult, and it is believed that he may have suffered from dementia at the end of his life. He also suffered a heart attack in 1997 that prevented him from making any additional public appearances. Barbara did take good care of him, however, and the two lived a relatively quiet existence in Los Angeles. Finally, on May 14, 1998, Sinatra passed away in Los Angeles. His death was marred by the fact that Barbara had failed to inform Frank's children of their father's impending death, leaving them unable to bid him one last farewell. Naturally, Sinatra's funeral was quite grand and included many luminaries, with more than 400 attendees in total.

Frank Sinatra is in many respects quintessentially American. His rise to fame is every bit the American Dream, and he remains a pop culture fixture. It has been argued that Sinatra was one of three figures who dominated specific eras throughout the first two-thirds of the twentieth century, with the other two being Bing Crosby (an influential figure for Sinatra himself) and Elvis Presley. Sinatra's fame with bobbysoxers in the early 1940s also made him a precursor to James Dean and the many young male heartthrobs who have since risen to fame. Most of all, his iconic status in American culture is cemented by the popularity of his songs, with songs like "New York, New York," "Chicago," and "Come Fly with Me" continuing to be featured at significant cultural events.

But at the same time, Sinatra is also iconoclastic. Sinatra's own life often contradicted the upbeat and prosperous image of America that his songs embraced. Sinatra was prone to bouts of depression, he was occasionally suicidal, he cheated on every woman he loved, and he was vindictive to anyone who he thought did him wrong. To an extent, some of the rougher aspects of Sinatra's life have actually become glorified themselves. That has all but assured Sinatra will continue to retain a unique position in American pop culture.

Bibliography

Fuchs, Jeanne & Prigozy, Ruth. Introduction. *Frank Sinatra: The Man, the Music, the Legend*. New York: Hofstra University Press, 2007. 1-6.

Fuchs, Jeanne. "Frank Sinatra: Dancer." *Frank Sinatra: The Man, the Music, the Legend*. New York: Hofstra University Press, 2007. 107-116.

Kael, Pauline. "The Man with the Golden Arm." *5001 Nights At the Movies*. New York: Owl Books, 461-462.

Kaplan, James. *Frank: The Voice*. New York: Random House, 2010.

McKinnon, Shaun, & Berns, Dave. "Sinatra Survived Yearlong Probe to Gain Gaming License." *Las Vegas Review-Journal* 17 May 1998.

McNally, Karen. *When Frankie Went to Hollywood: Frank Sinatra and American Male Identity*. Champagne: University of Illinois Press, 2008.

Rojek, Chris. *Frank Sinatra*. Cambridge: Polity Press, 2004.

Sinatra, Nancy. *Frank Sinatra: My Father*. Portland: Pocket, 1986.

Taraborrelli, J. Randy. *Sinatra: Behind the Legend*. Secaucus: Carol Publishing Group, 1997.

Turner, John F. Boulder: Taylor Trade Publishing, 2004.

Wild, David. "They Can't Take the Away from Me: Frank Sinatra and His Curious but Close Relationship with the Rock 'n' Roll Generation." *Frank Sinatra: The Man, the Music, the Legend*. New York: Hofstra University Press, 2007. 37-44.

Dean Martin

Chapter 1: Early Years

"Motivation is a lot of crap." – Dean Martin

All Americans are familiar with the name Dean Martin, but it was a name that he adopted only after entering show business. Dino Paul Crocetti was born on June 7, 1917, the son of Italian immigrants. His father Gaetano (Guy) was from Montesilvano, a small village on the coast of the Adriatic Sea, while his mother Angela was of Neapolitan and Sicilian descent. Gaetano arrived at Ellis Island in 1913, and Angela arrived one year later, but they married in 1914 when they were still just kids. Gaetano was 20 and Angela was just 16. They also wasted little time starting a family, with their first son Bill coming before Dino.

Martin and his parents

Employment prospects were relatively slim for Gaetano; who didn't have the formal education required for a good job. Like many of his Italian compatriots, he left New York and headed west, stopping at Steubenville, Ohio. At the time, Steubenville was a focal point of the steel industry; thanks to its location just 35 miles away from Pittsburgh, the steel capital of the United States. Steubenville was an industrial hotbed for manufacturing, which may not have made for a glamorous line of work but needed all the help it could get. As a farmhand from Italy, Gaetano was accustomed enough to manual labor, and his two older brothers had already arrived in Ohio. It was a foregone conclusion that Gaetano would join them.

Angela's background differed substantially from that of her future husband. She was raised by

German nuns, and though she held a strong sense of national pride, her upbringing had been more tranquil than her husband's. She was quiet, especially compared to her son, and she opened her own business as a seamstress, working from home. Instead of moving to Steubenville upon arriving in the United States, she settled in Fernwood, Ohio, a town located roughly 200 miles away.

Although Gaetano worked in the steel mills immediately after arriving in Steubenville, he eventually became a barber, a profession for which he was passionate. He and Angela raised their family in Steubenville, and although the small city held a rough flavor, the family lived in a friendly working-class neighborhood. Describing Steubenville, Martin's son Ricci explained the mix between congeniality and hard labor that typified the citizens: "Its residents mixed heartland patriotism with scraped knuckles and a dirt-under-the-fingernails work ethic. And at the end of the day, they knew how to have a good time." The town was far from affluent, but Gaetano's barber shop was a fixture, and the steady stream of scraggly steel mill workers provided constant business.

Gaetano and Angela raised their family with a strong sense of national pride. In fact, Italian was the spoken language in their household, and Dean did not learn English until after starting school. He entered Grant Elementary school in Steubenville, and he went on to attend Steubenville High School. From the beginning, Dean was never a strong or committed student, possibly due in large part to the fact that he could barely speak English when he began his education. His lack of familiarity made him an easy target for ridicule, as he was routinely chided for his bad English throughout elementary school. Finally, in the 10th grade, Martin quit school altogether, ending his education at Steubenville High. Always a wisecrack, Martin quipped that he was smarter than his teachers anyway.

Most descriptions of Martin's education cast his childhood in an excessively negative light. While he was certainly no scholar, Dean's upbringing was generally healthy and supportive. Not only was his biological extended family close-knit, but his neighborhood was close-knit and essentially doubled as a second family. As a child, Martin pursued a variety of hobbies, including playing bocce ball, singing in a choir, and being a boy scout. For better or worse, Martin's proclivity for leisure, something that would become a hallmark of sorts, played a strong role in precluding active engagement in his formal education. Instead of studying, he would go to watch movies, spend time in pool-rooms, and frequent nightclubs. The late 1920s and 1930s were a period of rapid growth in the motion picture industry, and Martin was as captivated as the rest of the nation. Films had just entered the era of synchronized sound, and in a sense Martin was able to better perfect his still-deficient English by watching films instead of in a more formal classroom environment, where his shoddy English was fodder for ridicule.

Martin's parents were able to tolerate their son dropping out of high school by placing a premium on hard work and impressing upon him the necessity to enter the workforce. Gaetano had always hoped his son would join him at the barber shop, but Dean was not exactly thrilled by that prospect. For a short time, he worked in the steel industry, which seems comical in retrospect, and it is unsurprising that he could not handle the brutal labor. He quit that job quickly, and he spent the remainder of his teenage years pursuing a variety of jobs that were loosely affiliated with the entertainment industry. He even took up boxing as a 15 year old, despite being just 135 pounds, fighting under the nickname "Kid Crochet", a play off his last name. He stuck at it long enough to batter his hands and suffer a broken nose, but he was so wildly unsuccessful that he later joked that he fought 12 times and "won all but 11" of them. One humorous legend claims that he would take money to box with his roommate and future Italian-American hit singer Sonny King in their apartment until one of them was knocked out.

Sonny King

Eventually, Martin worked as a roulette stickman and croupier in an illegal casino, which seems like a natural fit for him since the members of the Rat Pack were notorious for frequenting gambling establishments. Nonetheless, it's remarkable that Dean was able to secure such employment even at such a young age. He later said of his work, "I can't stand an actor or actress who tells me acting is hard work. It's easy work. Anyone who says it isn't never had to stand on his feet all day dealing blackjack."

Chapter 2: A Natural for Show Business

"Milton Berle is an inspiration to every young person that wants to get into show business. Hard work, perseverance, and discipline: all the things you need...when you have no talent." – Dean Martin

For the most part, the first two decades of Martin's life were not productive. His fun-loving personality was endearing to those around him, but he did not commit himself to either his studies or his jobs. Thankfully, that all changed beginning in 1934, when he began performing music for the first time.

During the summer of that year, Martin performed at Craig Beach, Ohio, and from the start he showed a great deal of talent and charisma. By this point in his career, Martin had not yet developed his style, but like Sinatra, he borrowed from the crooning musical styles of singers like Harry Mills and Bing Crosby. Even though his singing career was still in its beginning stages, Martin had an innate ability to charm an audience; he was extraordinarily good looking, and his pronounced Italian accent was a natural fit for the Ohioan demographic.

Bing Crosby

Martin continued to sing during summers while he worked as a boxer and roulette stickman, but he increasingly viewed those as temporary odd jobs on the way to being a singer. In the spring of 1939, his career began to take off after he performed at the Mounds Club in Lake County, Ohio. Performing for a wider audience earned him greater attention, and he was subsequently hired to join the Ernie McKay band in Columbus, his first major break.

When he was hired by the Ernie McKay band, he was instructed to change his name to "Dino Martino," a title that played off the fame of the Metropolitan Opera singer Nino Martini. There is no denying that "Dino Martini" has a catchier ring to it than Dino Crocetti, but the new designation still retained his Italian ethnicity. The new name conferred a certain exoticism to his image, but it still did so within the relatively narrow constraints of an explicitly Italian identity. It was also in keeping with his laid-back and fun-loving reputation, as the last name certainly reminded listeners of the drink too.

Performing with the Ernie McKay band was a major career development for Martin, but the following year his career reached even greater significance. In 1940, he was discovered by Sammy Watkins and eventually hired to join the Sammy Watkins Orchestra. However, Watkins did not care for the name "Dino Martini", and when he hired Crocetti in the fall of 1940, he insisted that the singer change his name to the very Americana "Dean Martin". The 23 year old had just been given his famous name.

Immediately after joining the Sammy Watkins orchestra, Martin performed with the group in the Cleveland area. Over time, he would perform on the road with the band, and they played all over the country. Signing with Watkins brought Martin his highest-ever salary, earning what was then a healthy $50 per week.

Martin's burgeoning career also corresponded with developments in his personal life. While singing in Cleveland, he met Betty MacDonald, a young lady from Swarthmore, Pennsylvania who was staying with her father in Cleveland. McDonald was just out of high school when she first met Dean. A strong, athletic woman who had been a lacrosse star, Betty's Irish heritage was obviously different than Martin's Italian background, but Martin was not deterred by her background. At the time, the Irish were held in equal if not higher regard than Italians, and Martin did not share the fierce Italian patriotism held by many immigrants and first-generation Italian-Americans. Never a shy gentleman, Martin courted her immediately, proposed to her just a few weeks after meeting her, and married here in Cleveland in October 1941. The couple took up residency in Cleveland Heights.

The itinerant lifestyle of the musical performer made domestic life especially difficult for the young couple. When Dean went off on extended road trips, Betty was left with little to keep her occupied. But in 1942, she and Martin had their first child when Stephan (later known as Craig) was born that summer. Martin's career also experienced a significant milestone in 1942, when he performed with the Sammy Watkins Orchestra for NBC on their broadcast of the "Fitch Bandwagon." It was the first time a national audience got a view of Martin, but he was still not making a great deal of money, a situation exacerbated by the fact his family was growing.

Martin in 1943

It has long been speculated that Martin's early singing career was helped in large part by connections to the Mafia, including with Chicago boss Sam Giancana. Entire books have been written on the alleged relationship between Martin and the mob. Characterizations of Martin's ties to the Chicago mob have ranged from being considered nonexistent to a big reason he got his break in show business. As with Sinatra, it's likely the truth was somewhere in-between; it was possible for Italian-Americans to have a friendly relationship with goodfellas and not be part of the mob.

Martin's career received another big boost when he was hired by the MCA talent agency in 1943. With that, he was able to perform at greater venues than before, finally acquiring the type of broad audience that facilitated national acclaim. Moreover, Martin became his own entity, freeing himself from the inherent restrictions of performing in a group. At long last, he was free to perfect his style in whichever way he saw fit. Around the same time, Frank Sinatra had become the most famous singer in America, and he had also broken out on his own in 1943, making what was then a virtually unprecedented move by performing as a soloist. In this vein, Martin's early career effectively mirrored Sinatra. Although he was not releasing any records (while Sinatra was), Martin's elevating stardom certainly owed a great deal to his future Rat Pack partner-in-crime.

From the beginning, Martin offered a fresh alternative to Sinatra. Although Sinatra had begun his career as a crooner, he transitioned to more showy tunes at a time in which Martin was perfecting the crooning style that would make him famous. Martin was also more visibly Italian than Sinatra, due to his swarthier skin complexion and far more pronounced accent. The two were similar, however, in that neither was formally trained as a singer and could not read sheet music.

Martin and Sinatra

Martin's early years as a solo performer were not entirely successful, however, In 1943, he was called upon to perform at the prestigious Riobamba club in New York City, and since he was still considered a relatively minor talent, he was a last-minute replacement for Sinatra. Unfortunately, Martin became overwhelmed by the situation, and his performance was an enormous failure. In retrospect, this performance is surprising since it is difficult to even envision Martin in a nervous state. In fact, his image as a relaxed, half-drunk but nevertheless charming performer was the result of years of familiarity performing before large audiences. To his credit, Martin continued to find steady employment even after the debacle.

By 1944, Martin had risen to the forefront of the entertainment industry. In January of that year, he appeared on the cover of *Billboard* magazine, and his calm façade was a refreshing antidote to the anxieties that filled wartime America. However, like many performers, Martin was drafted and called upon to serve in World War II in 1944. He was stationed in Akron, Ohio, but unbeknownst to him, Martin was suffering from a hernia at this time, and after just one year in the service he was classified as 4-F and discharged. Martin had never been enthusiastic about entering the service in the first place, and the discharge was a fortuitous development in his career. While other stars were off fighting overseas or training in the United States, Martin was able to work on his career and increase his popularity.

In March of 1944, Dean and Betty had a second child, a daughter named Claudia. Having a second child would suggest that Dean was becoming increasingly committed to being a family man, but in fact the exact opposite was true. As he became more famous, Martin had numerous affairs, and his traveling lifestyle offered the perfect opportunity for one-night stands. With legions of adoring fans, Martin had a captive audience, and his wife was not there to keep tabs on her husband. Martin's status as a poor family man surfaced in other ways too; he was irresponsible with the money he made and failed to adequately provide for Betty and the two children. The vast majority of the money he earned was spent immediately after it was received, forcing Betty to live frugally while her husband gallivanted around the country.

Martin's wife and kids weren't the only people who suffered from his financial mismanagement. In fact, after he signed with MCA, he decided to have a nose job to fix the damage done years earlier by boxing. However, he had been unable to save up the money to have the operation. He resorted to borrowing money for the operation, but then he spent the money he had borrowed. He got the nose job in August of 1944, but only after he had reached deals with so many talent agents that he had somehow managed to sign away over a substantial amount of his income.

Fortunately for Martin, his talent was able to compensate for his persistent inability to manage his funds. In August of 1944, shortly after getting his nose fixed, Martin was able to acquire his own radio show, a major accomplishment in an era in which the radio was just beginning to supplant cinema as the privileged form of entertainment in the United States. From the mid-1940s through the 1950s, more private forms of entertainment gained in popularity against the movie theater and baseball stadium. Even if it did not allow him to take advantage of his good looks, Martin's easy, crooning voice was a natural fit for the radio, and his fame only continued to grow.

Chapter 3: Martin and Lewis

Dean Martin and Jerry Lewis

Even as Martin continued to work in new ways, his financial situation did not improve. In 1945, he and Betty added a third child, Barbara Gail (known as Gail), but he was still not making a great amount of money. Of course, that didn't stop him from spending lavishly, and he even had to declare bankruptcy.

Nevertheless, Martin steadfastly projected a calm demeanor, and in 1946 his career changed dramatically. While performing at the Havana-Madrid in New York City, Martin began his professional partnership with Jerry Lewis.

The two had actually met the year before, and Lewis (in his suggestively-titled memoir *Dean and Me: A Love Story*) described his first encounter with Martin in terms that reflect awe and even voyeuristic wonder: "Just looking at him intimidated me: How does anybody get that handsome? I smiled at the sight of him in that camel's hair coat. Harry Horseshit, I thought. That was what we used to call a guy who thought he was smooth with the ladies…But this guy I knew, was the real deal."

Lewis' description captures the self-confident aura that Martin maintained, and it also hinted at the stark contrast between Martin and Lewis. Martin was Italian, suave, and traditionally masculine, while Lewis was Jewish and a bundle of frantic energy. Although the circumstances that initiated their partnership are unusual and purely coincidental, the natural contrasts between the two ensured a perfect and complementary comedic fit.

While at the Havana-Madrid, Martin was supposed to appear and sing. However, the nightclub owner actually needed a comedy duo more than a singer. Lewis was at large at the venue; he was not paid by the Havana-Madrid, but he hung around the club with regularity. On July 24, 1946, Martin and Lewis were called upon to perform together for the first time. Martin had no comedic acting experience, and for all of the appealing contrasts between the two, building a successful pairing typically takes a great deal of time. Predictably, their performance was met with derision, and later that night they overhauled their style completely. Instead of performing more "sophisticated" humor, they performed a purely improvised slapstick routine that won over the audience. Martin sang and dropped all pretense of being a serious comedian, while Lewis acted like a goof. Their comedy partnership was born.

Following their initial appearance together, Martin and Lewis reprised their routine and performed at the 500 Club in Atlantic City. Although they were billed separately, it was at the 500 Club that they first became acknowledged by the general public as a comedy duo. Their rise to fame was swift, and they began headlining programs and commanding salaries of $1200 per week. Their first performance as "Martin and Lewis" occurred at the Loew's State Theater in

New York City in 1947, where their weekly salary was $1500. By the following year, they commanded the extraordinary sum of $12,000 per week and were featured at elite venues like the Copacabana in New York City. Their performances set attendance records, and highbrow and lowbrow celebrities alike jockeyed for valuable seats in order to watch the duo in person, including silver screen icon Humphrey Bogart. To those who criticized his singing performances in the comedy routines, Martin shot back, "You wanna hear it straight, buy the album."

Bogart

That Dean Martin was able to achieve such fame with his comedy routine is remarkable, all the more so because his brand of acting was essentially to not act at all but rather to serve as the straight man to Jerry Lewis. The routine ensured that critics took more notice of Jerry Lewis, but considering that Martin never had any ambitions of being a comedic actor, the fact that he became part of the biggest comedy act in America was unprecedented. Lewis was certainly an awkward figure, but it made sense that he became famous as a comedian, because his brand of bodily humor was borrowed from a lineage of Yiddish humor predicated on physical slapstick. Thus, while he did not have the physical aura that surrounded Martin, his cultural background made him a more logical fit for success than Martin. Still, it is fair to wonder whether Martin and Lewis would have ever risen to fame without the other. As Lewis himself put it, "Who were Dean's fans? Men, women, the Italians. Who were Jerry's fans? Women, Jews, kids. Who were Martin and Lewis' fans? All of them... You had fans that didn't give a shit that Jerry was on or that Dean was singing. Because if Dean was singing, that was Martin and Lewis. If Jerry was goin' nuts, that was Martin and Lewis."

An early Martin and Lewis Performance

On August 19, 1948, Dean and Betty had their fourth child, Deana Martin, but once again the growing family belied the frictions between Martin and his wife. Betty grew increasingly exhausted by the constant affairs carried on by her husband (June Allyson and Rita Hayworth were among those he romanced during this period), and she was also left raising the children mostly by herself. In February of 1949, Dean told his family that he was going to leave them and asked that Betty acquiesce in granting him a divorce. At the time, he was entering into a relationship with Jeanne Bergier, an admiring fan who would frequent his performances, even on occasions in which Betty was in the audience. After Betty's refusal to grant a divorce (she still held out hope that they could reconcile their differences and salvage the marriage), Dean told her his mistress was pregnant. That compelled Betty to grant the divorce, and it was only later that she discovered Dean had fabricated the pregnancy in order to manipulate her into granting the divorce. Finally, in March of 1949, he and Betty finalized their divorce, and a few weeks later Martin began the longest-lasting of his three marriages by marrying Jeanne. Incredibly, Dean was granted custody of the children, subsidizing his ex-wife with alimony payments.

The aftermath of the divorce brought to light some of the shadier aspects of Martin's life. In particular, it has been suspected that he was aided by notorious gangster Anthony Fiato, who may have cheated Betty out of immense sums of alimony payments. Whether or not these rumors are true, they are part of the other allegations of mob connections held by Martin. Coincidentally or not, mobsters Sam Giancana and Tony Accardo may also have been affiliated with Frank Sinatra and the Rat Pack.

Over the course of the next decade, Martin's family expanded. In 1951, he and Jeanne had their first child, Dean Paul. Two years later, a second son, Ricci James, was born. Finally, in 1956, the couple added a third child, Gina Caroline. Martin quipped, "I've got seven kids. The three words you hear most around my house are 'hello,' 'goodbye,' and 'I'm pregnant." Martin was not an ideal father, and he had difficulty connecting with his children, but he maintained a constant presence in the household and his life was actually quite ordinary. In his memoir, Ricci Martin portrays his father in very normal terms, writing, "Because of the gallivanting image he had in the early movies and then later crystallized with Frank Sinatra and the Rat Pack, I think people have this image of him never being home. Instead, he tended to treat his stardom as any other 9-to-5 job. Actually, it was more like an 8-to-4 job."

Even as he grew increasingly famous due to his comedy performances with Jerry Lewis, Martin continued his singing career. In 1946, he recorded singles with Diamond, Apollo, and Embassy Records, and while the songs did not achieve any great acclaim, they did not end Martin's career as a singer either. In 1948, he and Lewis signed with Capitol Records, where they recorded a hit song, "That Certain Party."

Despite his brief stint singing alongside Lewis, Martin's singing career was predominantly as a soloist. In 1949, he experienced a major breakthrough after recording the hit song "Powder Your Face with Sunshine." The song reached number 10 on the charts, and though the lyrics never deviated far from the title, the song combined the cheery good feeling and cool suaveness that were present throughout his most famous songs. Over the following four years, he recorded over 80 sides, and in 1953, he recorded one of his most famous songs, the iconic "That's Amore". That song had been recorded for *The Caddy*, a film starring Martin and Lewis. "That's Amore" was a major milestone in his career, as it has been appropriated as a caricature of Italian culture. One of the most compelling aspects of Martin's rendition of it is the way in which he performs hyperbolically emotive lyrics in a cool, masculine manner. In 1954, Martin released his first two albums: *Dean Martin Sings* and *Swingin' Down Yonder*.

The beginning of the 1950s also saw significant developments in his partnership with Jerry Lewis. In 1949, the duo signed a contract with Paramount Studios. By this point, they were enormously popular within the entertainment industry, and they had the benefit of not being tied to the kind of contractual obligations that plagued most actors during the time period. By the end of the 1940s, the studio system was still very much in place in Hollywood; most actors effectively served as indentured servants, forced to appear in whichever films their parent studio decided and typecast as the studio saw fit. For the most part, Martin and Lewis were slated to appear in films directed by Hal Willis, but they were also given the freedom to appear in one outside film each year. Even better, they were allowed control over all of their other entertainment appearances. The leverage they had garnered from their fame performing live thus ensured a very comfortable arrangement within the motion picture industry, and they enjoyed privileges that were unheard of for all other actors just entering the film industry.

The first film for Martin and Lewis was *My Friend Irma* (1949), a largely forgotten film that featured Martin as Steve, a singer who falls in love with a money-loving woman and must also contend with Lewis' character. The first significant film for the duo was *Sailor Beware*, another Hal Willis film that featured Martin and Lewis as Al and Melvin, sailors who meet in the Navy recruiting line. Al has previously been rejected from the service due to his bad knees, while Melvin enters the service because he is allergic to women's fragrances and is ordered by a doctor to acquire sea travel. They are each admitted into the Navy, and the plot features the basic template for the Martin and Lewis films of the decade. Dean and Jerry act like a couple, with Martin playing the role of the virile man and Lewis the almost infantile son (or spouse). *Sailor Beware* also placed great emphasis on the striking physical, intellectual, and cultural differences between the pair. Constantly stuttering and stumbling about, Lewis appears very much as the Jewish comic, while Martin fulfills his image as the suave Italian. As the narrative progresses, Martin facilitates Lewis's maturation into the role of the confident heterosexual male. Much of the comedy in the films was based on the unlikelihood of Lewis ever attracting the women with whom he comes into contact in the films, but viewers were persuaded to gaze in wonder at his remarkable growth into the role of ladies man.

The following year saw the release of arguably Martin and Lewis's most famous film together, *The Caddy* (1953). The film was just the second (after *At War with the Army* (1950)) that was produced by York Pictures Corporation, a production company that Dean and Jerry had purchased at the start of the decade. Directed by Norman Taurog, the film features Martin as Joe, a golfer who benefits from the advice of Harvey (Lewis), the son of a famous golf professional. Harvey caddies for Joe, but later in the film, they decide to go into show business together, where they eventually meet the real-life Martin and Lewis. The plot contains some biographical elements, including the sheer coincidence that brought Dean and Jerry together as performers. The film is also highlighted by a show stopping production of "That's Amore," which became an immediate sensation. Moreover, the film is significant for exposing their actual personas; it was exceedingly rare for a film to make reference to the actual persona of the actors performing the characters. That the film "breaks the fourth wall" reflects the confidence the studio held in the Martin and Lewis brand, as well as the brand status wielded by the duo.

Martin and Lewis in *The Caddy*

Even as their cultural status continued to elevate, Martin and Lewis remained as prolific as ever through the mid-1950s. In 1955, they appeared in two films that did quite well at the box office, but one is considerably more acclaimed today than the other. First, they acted together in *You're Never Too Young* (1955), in which Jerry appears as Wilbur Lewis, a young man who pretends to be 11 years old in order to receive the children's price for the train fare. While on the train, he meets and falls in love with a schoolteacher who mistakes him for a child and gives him attention. Martin appears in the film as Bob Miles, fiancée to Nancy. The film is relatively minor within Martin's personal filmography; it is clear that Lewis is the main character, and Martin's role as straight man is largely ceded to the schoolteacher. At the same time, however, *You're Never Too Young* marked a turning point in the Dean and Jerry films. Unlike most of their other films, they both compete for the love of the same woman, and the Jerry-Dean partnership no longer exists to nurture Lewis' transformation into a man capable of courting a female. Lewis retains his trademark infantilism, but unlike the earlier films, the viewer gets the distinct impression that Martin's appearance in the film is largely tangential.

The more revered film in 1955 was *Artists and Models*, which stands alongside *The Caddy* in discussions of the most renowned of the Martin and Lewis films. Dean appears as Rick, a painter and ladies man, while Jerry appears as Eugene, Rick's roommate. As in their earlier film, the two characters are polar opposites. Rick is suave and calm, but Eugene conveys a constant, frantic energy. Rick's job as a painter aligns him with traditional "higher" forms of art, but Eugene is obsessed with comic books, which were regarded as more of a juvenile obsession than they are today. That the two characters are devoted to forms of graphic art is significant, as the film's highly-saturated colors and overall lavish visual style assume a comic book (or paint canvas) quality.

The plot of *Artists and Models* harkens back to the pre-*You're Never Too Young* films between the pair, as Dean assumes the role of partner and caretaker for the hyper Lewis. In fact, Lewis' sense of space and scale throughout the film is even more disorderly than in the earlier films. He relies on Martin in the manner that a pet relies on his owner, and an improbable romance develops between Eugene and the female comic book author who lives in their building due in large part to Rick's influence. At the same time, *Artists and Models* is similar to *You're Never Too Young* in that it subordinates Martin to focus on Lewis. In earlier films, Martin was permitted to assume equal or even greater prominence than his co-star, like with his arresting performance of "That's Amore" in *The Caddy*, but as the 1950s progressed, friction grew between the duo as Martin became acutely aware that he was essentially a straight-guy sidekick to the star attraction of Jerry Lewis. Exacerbating this dynamic was the close relationship that surfaced between Lewis and Frank Tashlin, a pairing that in many ways replaced the partnership between Martin and Lewis. In fact, Lewis and Tashlin would appear in a number of films throughout the 1950s and the first half of the 1960s, while Dean and Jerry acted alongside one another in just two more films.

Martin and Lewis in *Artists and Models*

The final two movies starring Martin and Lewis were both released in 1956. In *Pardners*, the duo star as ranchers who join forces to avenge the deaths of their fathers at the hands of a group of killers. In the context of their careers, *Pardners* was far more significant for Lewis than for Martin. Martin and Lewis both play two roles, appearing as parents and the (grown) children bent on bringing their fathers' killers to justice. Although the dual roles (as fathers and then sons) are highly similar, the film was the first in a long line of movies in which Lewis performs separate roles (the most famous among these is *The Nutty Professor*, in which Lewis' alter ego character borrows heavily from Martin himself.)

The last film starring Martin and Lewis was *Hollywood or Bust* (1956), a film that features a heavy autobiographical subtext. Dean and Jerry star as Steve and Malcolm. They each win the same car, Malcolm legitimately and Steve via a fake ticket. It is decided that they will share the winning car, but they have conflicting agendas concerning what they should do with it. Eventually, they drive to Hollywood at Malcolm's behest, where he endeavors to meet Anita Ekberg (and eventually does.) *Hollywood or Bust* characterized the majority of their earlier films, and the two characters travel to Hollywood the same way Dean and Jerry traveled to Hollywood together.

By 1956, the relationship between Martin and Lewis was breaking down. It was understandable that Martin was irritated about playing second fiddle to Lewis, but he also accused Lewis of changing. Martin said of Lewis, "At some point, he said to himself, 'I'm extraordinary, like Charles Chaplin.' From then on, nobody could tell him anything. He knew it all." In one legendary exchange, Martin told Lewis that Lewis was "nothing but a f****** dollar sign" to him. Their partnership ended 10 years to the day that they had formally teamed up.

Chapter 4: Moving On

When Martin split from Lewis, there was little doubt that he would continue to remain popular, but the public wanted to see if his persona would change. He had long been seen as a crooning straight man to Lewis's zaniness, but he possessed the good looks and an athletic frame that lent itself to all kinds of film roles. Martin also wanted to be viewed as a more serious actor.

Martin's first film without Lewis was *Ten Thousand Bedrooms* (1957). He played a wealthy hotel owner who abuses his staff, but eventually he falls in love and the film ends (as most Hollywood films of the time do) with a successful romance. Interestingly, the film was both prophetic with regard to his late career but also wildly unsuccessful. In his review of the film, *The New York Times* critic Bosley Crowther had difficulty accepting Martin without his former comedic collaborator, noting that he was "just another nice-looking crooner without his comedy pal. Together, the two made a mutually compatible team. Apart, Mr. Martin is a fellow with little humor and a modicum of charm." This sentiment reflects the way in which *Ten Thousand Bedrooms* was likely not the proper film for Martin to appear in while attempting to extricate himself from his professional marriage with his former co-star. In particular, the film veered too close to the brand of over-the-top comedy that had characterized his earlier films. Martin retained the charm of his earlier roles and displayed the ability to play a romantic lead, but the script was comedic and he lacked a rowdy character that would contrast with his detached, calm demeanor. It likely would have been more opportune for Martin to appear in a more serious film that would have allowed viewers to observe him in an entirely fresh light.

Fortunately for Martin, his next films were the perfect antidotes to the harsh reviews that his last film received. Martin's next film was *The Young Lions* (1958), a film that is largely forgotten today but performed an invaluable function in resurrecting his career. In the film, he played the role of Michael Whiteacre, a cowardly man who grows more courageous over the course of the narrative. The film is very much a product of the 1950s. First, the running time was an epic 167 minutes, far longer than the relatively brief Martin and Lewis films. The lengthiness also reflected Hollywood's emphasis on lengthy epics, which was a response to the industry's need to distinguish itself from the increasingly severe threat of television. Finally, it is also significant that the film was directed by Edward Dmytryk, an extreme-left director with strong Popular Front connections. While the film is not particularly overt in its political affiliations, it was significant that Martin agreed to appear in a film directed by such a political maverick.

Martin's public image also benefitted from his co-stars in *The Young Lions*, Montgomery Clift and Marlon Brando. Although Brando had lost a degree of his luster with the emergence (and then death) of James Dean, he was still an enormous star within the industry, and appearing alongside him was a tremendous boost of credibility for a struggling Martin. Meanwhile, Montgomery Clift's image was less secure than Brando's. Just two years before, he had been involved in a disastrous car accident that left him with facial wounds. However, there was no doubting his acting presence, and he and Brando both epitomized the Method acting style that had been popularized during the previous decade by Lee Strasberg at the Actors Studio. The Method approach, which borrowed heavily from Stravinsky, emphasized an emotive approach in which the actor displays no personal trademarks but instead absorbs themselves completely into their role. It is easy to see how Martin would have been attracted to this approach, especially at a time when he was faced with the challenging task of disassociating himself from Lewis. Appearing in a war drama with Method actors was about as far removed as he could get from his earlier films, and it exposed viewers to a versatility they didn't know Martin possessed.

Montgomery Clift

Marlon Brando

Martin's image also evolved through his association with the Rat Pack, a group of Las Vegas entertainers who promoted an image of easy living and hedonistic consumption. Always a fun-loving man who had enjoyed gambling and alcohol, Martin was a natural fit with the fun-loving group, joining entertainment luminaries Frank Sinatra, Peter Lawford, Sammy Davis, Jr., Joey Bishop, Angie Dickinson, and Shirley MacLaine. Martin made light of his image as a laid-back but smooth womanizer who was always half in the bag, joking, "I drink because my body craves, needs alcohol. I don't drink, my body's a drunk." He also had no problem cracking wise about his own friends, saying of Shirley MacLaine, "Shirley, I love her, but her oars aren't touching the water these days."

Martin effectively swapped his association with the infantile Jerry Lewis for a more glamorous affiliation with members of the entertainment elite. He began performing at the Sands nightclub, where he held an ownership stake, and after befriending Sinatra and the other members of the group, Martin also became more political. For example, he barnstormed for John F. Kennedy in the 1960 presidential election.

Considering the new look to the Martin image offered by *The Young Lions*, it is perhaps surprising that his next film was far different than that war film. Released in 1958, Martin appeared in *Some Came Running*, directed by acclaimed Hollywood director Vincente Minnelli. The film stars Frank Sinatra as an alcoholic writer who has returned from the army, while Martin appears as his fun-loving friend, an alcoholic named Bama. Martin's role is relatively insignificant compared to Sinatra's part, but it established the precedent for most of his later film appearances. Martin was a natural as a hedonistic, pleasure-seeking individual, but *Some Came Running* is memorable mainly for Sinatra's bravura performance as a veteran struggling to integrate back into society following his time in the service. Nevertheless, Martin's later performances would borrow heavily from his appearance in that film.

Building on the acclaim of his past two films, Martin next appeared in *Rio Bravo* (1959), the film that is generally regarded as the most acclaimed of his career. It also gave him the opportunity to work with Howard Hawks, whose playful energy worked well with Martin. *Rio Bravo* built on the trend toward revising old genres. *Rio Bravo* is one of the most famous Westerns, but at the same time it veers away from the kind of classic Westerns directed by John Ford and even Hawks himself earlier in his career. The basic plot involves an eclectic community attempting to ward off a vengeful man attempting to free his brother from imprisonment.

Martin in *Rio Bravo*

On the surface, *Rio Bravo* appears very much a stereotypical Hollywood Western. Not only does it star John Wayne (rivaled only by Clint Eastwood as an icon of the genre), but the nearly 2 ½ hour running time was right up there with the epics of the decade. Additionally, the revenge-driven good guy vs. bad guy plot is central to most Westerns. However, despite its length, the film could not be further removed from the orthodox Western. While most films in the genre contain action-packed plots and dramatic views of wide vistas (John Ford's beloved Monument Valley being the archetypal example), *Rio Bravo* contains very little plot activity. The narrative plods along at a protracted pace, to the point that boredom becomes one of the principal motifs of the film. The people defending the town (the "good guys") could not be more dissimilar, and as the narrative progresses they learn to adopt a collectivist stance that eventually defeats the opposition. The apparent incongruity of John Wayne, Ricky Nelson, Dean Martin, Walter Brennan, and Angie Dickinson starring alongside one another also becomes resolved as they learn to appreciate and make use of their stark differences, culminating in a bizarre "team effort" shootout at the conclusion.

Beyond its basic plot, one of the more compelling aspects of *Rio Bravo* is the biographical resonance that surrounds each of the main characters. Martin plays an alcoholic named Dude (nicknamed Borrachon due to his drinking habit), who previously served as sheriff's deputy to Chance (played by John Wayne.) At the start of the film, Dude's alcoholism leaves him in a pathetic state, not only unable to defend his town but also himself. Over the course of the film, he achieves sobriety and reacquires his pinpoint shooting accuracy and broader sense of dignity. John Wayne's character is also in keeping with his star image, as he must overcome his trademark individualism and learn to cooperate with others. By the late 1950s, Martin had become widely viewed as a functioning alcoholic committed more to his easygoing lifestyle than any sense of professional or familial obligation, and his character in *Rio Bravo* effectively combats this image. Casting Martin as an alcoholic was hardly unusual, as he had just portrayed one in *Some Came Runnning*, and he would continue to be cast as one in later films, but this film frames Martin's public persona in a tragic light. Dude (Borrachon) is not the suave, tipsy figure who appears in *Some Came Running* but is instead depicted as a sad individual whose alcoholism hinders his marksmanship and worth. The narrative is one of redemption, prompting Robin Wood to state, "*Rio Bravo* remains, beyond politics, as a (political?) argument as to why we should all go on living and fighting."

In the wake of *Rio Bravo*, Martin worked with Minnelli once again, appearing alongside Judy Holliday in the film adaptation of the Broadway hit *Bells are Ringing* (1960). Considering his singing talents, it is surprising that Martin was not cast in more musicals during his career, but he rarely appeared in MGM films, the studio known for its musicals. Besides, MGM already had a stable roster of musical actors at their disposal.

After *Bells are Ringing*, Martin strengthened his affiliation with the Rat Pack, appearing in *Ocean's Eleven* (1961) and *Robin and the Seven Hoods* (1964). Of the two films, *Ocean's Eleven* has had a significantly greater impact, inspiring a host of Hollywood sequels decades later. Directed by Lewis Milestone, the film features the Rat Pack involved in a major series of heists robbing five Las Vegas casinos. The film appears almost antithetical to *Rio Bravo*, and this is true to an extent. While it should be noted that *Ocean's Eleven* is similar to the earlier film because it has Martin essentially playing himself, *Rio Brava* casts a negative light on his lifestyle while *Ocean's Eleven* glamorizes the easy-living of the Rat Pack.

Martin's image as a leisurely, hard-drinking entertainer ensured that he stayed famous, but it also had the negative effect of limiting the range of characters he was given in films. His image as a middle-aged slacker who enjoys having a good time did give him a certain niche, but that niche did not lend itself to the hardworking ethos of the male star. Ultimately, Martin had the handsome physical appearance of a leading actor, but his image was antithetical to the hard-working, progress-driven ethos of most films. As a result, he continued to appear in films in which he essentially portrayed himself. In 1964, he acted in *Kiss Me Stupid*, directed by the famous Billy Wilder. The biographical bent of his character is unmistakable, as Martin portrays a pleasure-loving crooner named Dino. Martin did not diversify his acting range, but he solidified this character type to the point that it essentially became a brand.

In the mid-1960s, Martin became even more active with his singing career and actually achieved greater popularity than he had during his early career. 1964 was a particularly successful year with the release of three of Martin's most famous songs: "Everybody Loves Somebody," "The Door is Still Open to My Heart," and "You're Nobody Till Somebody Loves You." All three songs reached number one on the Adult Contemporary charts, while "Everybody Loves Somebody," reached number one overall. Listening to the songs, there is no significant difference in singing style from his earlier songs; in fact, "Everybody Loves Somebody" was written in 1947. It's puzzling that Martin's career as a singer did better after several decades, but it was a result of the man's reputation himself instead of any change in style. At a time in which popular music had gravitated toward folk music, and with the British Invasion already underway, Martin offered a throwback to an earlier period, and a seemingly more American one at that. What is remarkable about Martin is that by the 1960s, crooning had already become antiquated, and yet he was able to gain in popularity even while singing an outmoded style of music. No matter the circumstances, Martin's brand of "cool" never went out of style. Even while Rat Pack cohort Frank Sinatra modified his style in the 1960s, Martin continued along the same path unscathed.

Chapter 5: Late Career

Martin and Sinatra on *The Dean Martin Show*

Martin continued his prolific singing career from 1965-1975, often producing several songs a year, but he never achieved the popularity he had garnered earlier in the decade. Dean also continued to act in films, but he never returned to the melodramatic territory of *The Young Lions*. It's ironic that *The Young Lions* is largely responsible for resurrecting his film career, and yet he restricted himself to comedies and Westerns late in his career. In 1966, Martin starred in *The Silencers* (1966), a spy spoof that played on the popularity of the James Bond films. The film starred Martin as a retired secret agent who becomes involved in a plot concerning an atomic bomb in New Mexico. In the end, Martin's character defeats his nemesis and wins the girl. In spite of the formulaic plot, the film was a major box office success, and Martin would actually star in three loose sequels over the following four years: *Murderers' Row* (also released in 1966), *The Ambushers* (1967), and *The Wrecking Crew* (1968). None of the films were critically acclaimed, but the pace at which they were released attests to Martin's work ethic.

Late in his career, Martin starred in either Westerns, big-budget disaster films, or comedic spoofs of Westerns. In 1970, he appeared in *Airport*, the film that spawned the disaster-epic film and inspired a host of comedic variations of the subgenre. Surprisingly (given his age), Martin starred in the action-packed police drama *Mr. Ricco* in 1975, playing the role of a detective. The film borrowed from the success of *Dirty Harry* and *French Connection* (1971), although Martin was too old to properly inhabit the role. Otherwise, during the late 1960s and 1970s Martin predominantly appeared in Westerns, including *Texas Across the River* (1966), *Rough Night in Jericho* (1967), *5 Card Stud* (1968), and *Showdown* (1973). Considering that he was already past the age of 50 by the time that *Texas Across the River* was made, it is fair to wonder how he could be cast in such a rugged role. However, by the late 1960s and 1970s, the Western was aging as a genre, and casting older stars corresponded with the more middle-aged viewing demographic. Meanwhile, Western films starring younger actors, like the Spaghetti Westerns with Clint Eastwood and films like *Butch Cassidy and the Sundance Kid*, were revisionist Westerns geared toward a younger audience.

Although Martin continued to find steady employment as a singer and movie star, his most significant occupation during the late 1960s and early 1970s was as a television host. In 1965, *The Dean Martin Show* debuted, naturally featuring Martin as the show's host. On the show, Martin entertained stars and perfected his image as a half-drunk, middle-age playboy. During each show, he performed two musical numbers, one serious and the other more comedic, thereby fulfilling his most famous functions as a comedy actor and romantic crooner.

The show also gained publicity (and notoriety) for Martin's behavior, which occasionally probed the limits of risqué conduct. He routinely flirted with his female guests, offering quips that were loaded with sexual innuendo. Another signature of the show was the half-drunken glass of whiskey that was constantly at his side. Although it has been popularly alleged that the glass was often filled with apple juice, it served as a prop that reinforced the easy-living Las Vegas lifestyle of the Rat Pack. *The Dean Martin Show* was an immediate success, and in 1967 Martin signed a record contract with NBC that gave him $34 million over three years.

Martin and guest Florence Henderson on *The Dean Martin Show*

At a time in which television was gaining in popularity, *The Dean Martin Show* was able to distance itself from the competition by banking on Martin's star power. There were other popular shows, but Martin was the first singer and actor who seamlessly transitioned into television, and the opportunity to watch Martin perform two songs during each show was a major competitive advantage for the show, at least until Martin's charm began to wear away. In the early 1970s, the show declined in popularity as audiences grew tired of Martin's dated playboy image. One review from 1972 noted, "When was it that Dean Martin ceased to be in any way amusing?...the humor had been distilled from the sweat socks of junior high school hoodlets. The whole thing reminded me of acne." This review also reflected the influence of feminism and cultural studies, which had just begun to emerge. Martin's playboy act was suddenly deemed sexist and offensive, and the show was ended in 1974.

With the termination of *The Dean Martin Show*, Martin began to remake his image, shifting away from musical performances and more toward comedy. In 1974, he began a new show for NBC titled *The Dean Martin Celebrity Roast*. As with *The Dean Martin Show*, the episodes were predicated on a celebrity guest, but unlike the former show, Martin would "roast" the guest. The show was a hit and lasted until 1984. At a time in which he was scaling down in his film appearances and musical performances, *The Dean Martin Celebrity Roast* kept Martin in the public sphere. It also helped solidify his reputation in every respect, as the charming host roasted all kinds of individuals. Perhaps most ironically, given that he wasn't writing his own material, Martin once joked about Bob Hope, "As a young boy, Bob didn't have much to say. He couldn't afford writers then."

One of the more significant developments for Martin during the 1970s was his divorce from Jeanne, to whom he had been married for over 20 years. After filing for divorce, an unusual move for a husband, Martin joked, "I know it's the gentlemanly thing to let the wife file. But, then, everybody knows I'm no gentleman." In 1973, he married Catherine Hawn, a woman young enough to be his daughter. He was deeply committed to her at first and adopted her daughter Sasha, but the age gap between the two eventually rendered the marriage untenable. They divorced after three years.

By the turn of the 1980s, Martin entertainment career was concentrated almost exclusively on his show. He did appear in two over-the-top comedies, *The Cannonball Run* (1981) and *Cannonball Run II* (1984), but his film appearances were infrequent. Finally, after a run of roughly 10 years, *The Dean Martin Celebrity Roast* ended in 1984. Although Martin did not formally announce his retirement, he effectively retired when his show ended. The rest of his life would revolve around golf and leisure.

Martin with Sammy Davis, Jr., Shirley MacLaine, and Sinatra on the Set of *Cannonball Run II*

After the close of his show in 1984, Martin began a reclusive lifestyle that could not have been more different than the very public image of him as a glamorous Rat Pack icon. The public perception of Martin as an outgoing man was always largely inaccurate, but Martin became even more withdrawn in his later years. He enjoyed golfing and held memberships at the Bel Air and Riviera Country Clubs in California, but he otherwise spent the bulk of his time at home watching television. He rarely saw even his closest friends, and the man known for being a quintessential drinker hated to host parties or attend them.

By this point, Martin was rich, but he also made a series of wise real estate investments that added to his wealth and guaranteed his financial stability. On occasion, he performed in public, most notably when he appeared on a CBS Telethon with Jerry Lewis in 1976 at the behest of Sinatra. That brought about a public reconciliation with his former co-star. In the early 1980s, the Rat Pack went on a reunion tour, but Martin clashed with Sinatra and the tour was not a success. His final shows were in 1989-1990 in Las Vegas.

Martin's reclusive nature surprised many, but he had always been more subdued than Jerry Lewis, Frank Sinatra, and his other show business partners. His wife Jeanne once noted, "No one, nothing impressed him deeply." Beneath his façade as an entertainer, Martin was a very simple man. While he enjoyed his liquor and was adept at promoting his image as a functioning alcoholic, he thrived on routine, and his prolific careers in singing, film and television show that he was truly a dedicated and hard worker.

The final decade of Martin's life was relatively somber. In March of 1987, his son Dean died in a plane crash. The death devastated him, and he was never able to shake off the lingering depression from the event. He became even more withdrawn and ventured outside his house even less (Ricci Martin). Subsequently, in 1993 Martin was diagnosed with lung cancer, and he announced his official retirement in 1995. The cancer transformed him into a skeletal figure during his final years, and he died on Christmas Day in 1995.

Analyzing Dean Martin's career can be a tough undertaking since he performed in a wide array of entertainment platforms and remained successful for such an extended period of time. At the same time, no matter the arena, Martin essentially appeared as the same figure, a laid-back Italian crooner who women fantasized over and men attempted to emulate. Thus, the central paradox of Martin's career is the manner in which it is both incredibly diverse and at the same time remarkably constant. In a sense, what differentiate Martin's films and entertainment productions from one another are not his own characters but the different actors with whom he was cast. In the Jerry Lewis films and in *The Dean Martin Show*, Martin essentially portrays the same suave, calm figure. The major difference lies in the fact that Jerry Lewis appears in one, while he occupies center stage in the other. Whether appearing alongside Jerry Lewis, Frank Sinatra, or by himself, Martin's own image remained relatively intact throughout his career.

Martin's personal life magnifies the stark contrast between his upbringing and the fame he later enjoyed. Indeed, it is almost unfathomable that a social outcast who was ridiculed for his accent and quit school altogether in the 10th grade could grow up to become such an entertainment legend. As a student and a young man, he was entirely unremarkable, and had Martin's career been unsuccessful, it is difficult to envision him achieving success in any other venue. At the same time, it is unlikely that his fame will ever disappear, and few stars are able to enjoy the wide appeal Dean Martin has had across many generations. As Bob Greene noted, "The coolness of Dean Martin seamlessly crosses generations; young guys heading for a weekend in Las Vegas with their buddies understand his appeal just as viscerally as their grandparents do."

Even if they were not always critically successful, Martin's enduring appeal ensures that his songs and films will forever remain culturally relevant.

Bibliography

Carnes, Mark C., ed. *American National Biography: Supplement 2*. Oxford: Oxford University Press, 2005.

Crowther, Bosley. "Ten Thousand Bedrooms." *The New York Times*. 4 April 1957. Retrieved from http://movies.nytimes.com/movie/review?res=9F00E2D61E3EE63ABC4C53DFB26683

8C649EDE.

Cyclops. "The Witless Reign of King Leer." *Life* 7 April 1972: 14.

Greene, Bob. "Why Dean Martin's Still So Cool." *CNN*. 8 April 2012. Retrieved from http://www.cnn.com/2012/04/08/opinion/greene-dean-martin.

Lewis, Jerry, & James Kaplan. *Dean and Me: (A Love Story)*. New York: Broadway Books, 2005.

Martin, Deana, and Wendy Holden. *Memories are Made of This: Dean Martin Through His Daughter's Eyes*. New York: Three Rivers Press, 2004.

Martin, Ricci. *That's Amore: A Son Remembers His Father*. Lanham: Taylor Trade Publishing, 2002.

Smith, John L. *The Animal in Hollywood: Anthony Fiato's Life in the Mafia*. New York: Barricade Books, 1998.

Tosches, Nick. *Dino: Living High in the Dirty Business of Dreams*. New York: Dell Publishing, 1992.

Wood, Robin. *Rio Bravo*. London: BFI, 2003.

Made in the USA
Middletown, DE
22 October 2023

41262902R00040